Dark Warrior

You're always on the right path.
Even when you're not.

David Walther

2QT Limited (Publishing)

Second Edition 2020

2QT Limited (Publishing)
Settle, North Yorkshire BD24 9BZ
United Kingdom

The author has his own website: www.davidwalther.co
Cover by Matt Brown

This story is woven together from some events that are real but might seem unreal and some events that are unreal but might seem real. Any resemblance to persons and places you know is entirely coincidental.

Printed by Amazon Inc

A CIP catalogue record for this book is available
from the British Library

ISBN 978-1-913071-82-0

Unsung Warrior

Much of this world is hidden from view
Only is seen by the chosen few
Do not be fretful of what you can't see
Be thankful instead that you are free

Battles are raging unseen all around
Up in the heavens and here on the ground
Be glad that you live out your life unaware
And that others have taken the challenge to care

Few are the Warriors here on the earth
They know their strength, their power and worth
Silent and strong, they defend our soul
To keep us together, in safety and whole

The demons are real, doubt at your cost
You know not when your soul may be lost
You may feel an inkling that something's not right
That's when you must call on a warrior to fight

A feeling inside of deep held unease
A feeling of being watched does you tease
Weakness of spirit or black cloudy mood
On sadness and sorrowful thoughts you may brood

Call on your guides to come to your aid
Throw up the best protection that you've made
Call in the light and ask Michael to speed
To your side he will come whenever there's need

Remember though if you feel unequipped
There are ways for the balance to be tipped
There are a few human warriors still
Who possess ancient wisdom, knowledge and skill

Do not despair and sink into gloom
The battle's not over, it's not all doom
You can be set free from demonic intent
And return to your previous life, be content

So stay now alert especially the pure
Stay free from the darkness' beckoning lure
Live in the light, shine bright in your soul
And remember your purpose, your path and your goal

Written By Sue Penney

Note from the Author

It's not important whether you believe that the contents of this book are true or not. What's important is that you get something from it, be it learning, your eyes opening, personal growth or just pure pleasure. What's important is that you read and enjoy, that you remain open to new things, you evolve, grow, and become more. Embracing change, looking at new ideas and concepts … that's how creativity and the advancement of the human race occur.

No one says you have to accept change. But sitting in your own bubble with your head stuck in the sand, seeing and hearing nothing, is the path to stagnation and to mediocrity at best.

The Big Picture

And so it is that the eternal battle of light versus dark continues. For while it is the very nature of opposing forces to challenge one another, vying for perceived dominance, there is a bigger picture involved. For it is during this conflict that creation occurs. It is through such conflict that entire worlds are born.

Indeed, the whole universe exists as a result of such conflict, from the birth of planets to the tiniest organism existing in the remotest part of the universe. Everything acts out this scene. Be it pure survival, or warlike conquest over others, it is all part of the great creation of all things. The ultimate grand plan of the universe.

Including us. *Homo sapiens*. People.

Just think about that for a moment. Just one moment. Mind-boggling, isn't it? So what do we do? We keep fighting is what we do. We fight for what we feel is right within our hearts. And hopefully, we grow, we evolve, we are. For we know no other way.

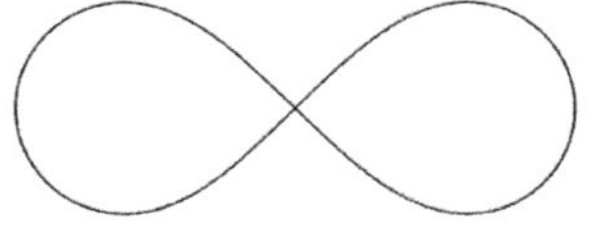

Prologue

Several Years Later
The Journey

Mark sat in his favourite coffee shop, pondering the events of the last few years. How much he had experienced and grown as a result.

While this may have been his life path, which, by the way, he firmly believed it was, events had unfolded to test him to the limits. But, during this time, though he had triumphed, the bigger picture was mind-boggling. Good versus evil. Darkness versus light.

Darkness had been beaten. For now. And he felt he had earned a temporary respite.

But he knew it would be exactly that. Temporary. What he had witnessed, in that room in London, was Belthazar finally showing his hand. Archangel Michael confronting Belthazar, potentially saving Mark's life, showed something else. This had been, and was, an ongoing battle. In which potentially, he was just a pawn. A pawn. That is what Belthazar had referred to him as on that fateful day.

Three years ago after dealing with a particularly malicious and protracted case against the dark he had travelled to a London retreat for a well earned rest. On arrival he had been ambushed by dark forces hoping to catch him unaware and had been forced to fight a long vicious hand to hand battle. Wading through the house with dark minions throwing themselves across his path from every quarter fully intent on destroying him. Having fought his way through he was finally confronted by Belthazar himself who supplied just enough information to piece together some of the bigger picture; just before he was about to wipe him out. Mark took a deep breath. Indeed, had Michael not appeared, Belthazar may well have succeeded. And then Michael himself had filled in yet more pieces of the puzzle. Enabling him to glean his most complete understanding yet.*

Dragging himself out from reminiscence about that black day, he stared at the coffee in his hand and thought for a moment.

No, not a pawn, he reasoned. A soldier. A weapon for the light.

His mind opened further, allowing him to see a bigger truth. He was a willing soldier. And had been born gifted and trained as such from birth. Things were falling together.

He thought back to everything he saw as a child. The dark shadows that had stalked him at night after his parents had put him to bed. Lying there, seeing dark shadows flitting across his vision, flowing around the room, hiding behind cupboard doors, curtains, the side of the bed. And him being terrified, trying desperately to manage his fear. Pretending to put up light shields around his bed in protection. Keeping out the monsters in his room that hunted him.

It was not until he was an adult that his parents told him he used to wake up screaming at night. They didn't know why. But he did now.

The monsters weren't in his imagination. They were real. Even then they were testing him. Attacking in the hours of darkness, when they are strongest, and you are at your weakest as you let your guard down and your spirit loosens in your physical body.

---

* Story recited in Book 1. The Diary of a Gatekeeper.

But still, at that tender young age and not knowing, he had automatically employed shields to protect himself. Keeping the monsters at bay.

So they had known. They had tried to deal with him while he was young and vulnerable. And they had failed.

And now he was aware.

Time had not stopped for Mark in the last few years since then, either. To be able to face his own demons he had been forced to grow and evolve. It had been a long, arduous journey, with much pain and emotional turmoil. In his quest for power and the ability to face even graver threats, he had turned more to the dark powers. Over a period of time he became more and more accustomed to fighting darkness with darkness and had become a master in that field. Because he was able to summon all kinds of dark beings at will, it became his default setting. And it worked.

But of course this was limited. Mark was a light being. There was a grave risk of using dark powers and beings, of falling into darkness himself and becoming lost. And a graver risk of being manipulated by the same dark forces as those he used for the greater good.

It was a perilous path to walk, and one that only the strongest could survive.

So spirit stepped in. And stripped Mark of his powers. The first sign was his inability to ground himself properly, on his feminine side. Never having had this problem before, he was confused. The energy seemed to bounce up and down like a yo-yo whenever he tried to channel it down his left side into or from the ground. This was accompanied by a general feel of unease. He was not happy within himself. Realising he was unbalanced somehow, Mark was forced to seek advice from learned teachers across the country.

Eventually he discovered the problem. Spirit informed him via a wise woman he met.

'You have become a master of fighting darkness with darkness. Now you must learn to use the light. Eventually you will become even more powerful. But that is in the future. To do this you must change within yourself. We cannot just give you new light powers. You must change and become more balanced, evolve and grow to a point within yourself where you can wield these new powers. Then, once you have mastered this, you will be able to access both light and dark and truly become who you were meant to be.'

Thereby a journey was started. Mark found he was stripped of his powers of darkness. He could see the dark beings off to the side in the middle distance. But they were separated behind a barrier of light. He could see and feel that they were willing, but unable, to reach him.

For the first time in his life Mark felt vulnerable. In a stage now where he was frequently required to fight and deal with malicious beings, he had been stripped of his powers. His swords and guns, so to speak, were gone. He felt truly defenceless. The dark forces were not slow in sensing his new vulnerability, and set to the attack almost immediately.

One such example happened during a regular day. While having a break from work, he had decided to look at a new housing development. After walking into the main office and speaking to the agent inside he was pointed in the direction of the show homes and encouraged to feel free to look around.

Mark set off down the short pathway outside and soon reached the house. He opened the front door to a three-bedroom show home. Once inside he noticed that it felt small and lacking in positive energy. Though prettily decorated, adorned with glossy new fixtures and fittings to draw in the customers, it just didn't feel right. As he walked up the stairs the feeling grew and Mark began to feel more uncomfortable. After looking around the two bedrooms and the bathroom on the first floor, he moved up to the third floor and the large extra room. The feeling of unease increased and he quickly decided he wanted to leave. Something was wrong here, and he knew it.

Walking down the first flight of stairs his feeling of unease turned to one of fear, and the hairs on the back of his neck stood on end. He knew without doubt now that a dark being was in the house and meant him harm. Increasing his pace, he crossed the landing and started to descend the last flight of stairs, while feeling the presence drawing ever closer. On reaching the halfway point down the staircase he could feel it almost upon him. Because he had been stripped of his powers, Mark was genuinely fearful. How could he fight them without his powers?

Mark turned to look, and saw it at the top of the stairs. A demon of considerable size and power was staring balefully down at him. Over six feet tall and totally black, its aura was almost as dense and black as its body. Sensing its apparent defenceless victim was almost within reach, its eyes glittered in triumph.

With a lunge the demon leapt forward. Almost simultaneously, a bright white presence appeared in front of Mark. Shining as bright as the demon was dark, the guardian angel raised her hands and an intense white light barrier appeared at the top of the stairs. The demon was stopped dead in its tracks. Pounding on the barrier, testing its strength, it stared down at its retreating victim with waves of dark energy emanating from it.

Mark wasted no time and moved swiftly down the rest of

the stairs and straight out of the front door, where he let out an enormous exhalation of air.

A sense of relief washed over him as the feeling of threat disappeared. After taking a few moments to gather himself, he thought about what had just happened. He hadn't been left completely defenceless. A new guardian angel had been given to him. And just in time.

And so this is how things continued. Mark was continually sent new challenges, which were always big enough to make him feel as though he would tip over the edge. But somehow he always managed to triumph. He was slowly evolving and growing. Always using light powers, and changing within.

He was stepping into his true light power, yet still becoming stronger. Recent events and transformations had taken him to a new level of ability. Gradually he became able to do things he had not been able to do before.

Yet still he knew there was more to come. Evolving should never stop. Just because you feel you have reached a certain level it doesn't mean you should stop striving for more. Mark passionately believed this.

And he knew he would need it. Darkness was coming. He could feel it in his bones, his very soul. And he knew, without doubt, he would need every ounce of extra power he could get.

This is his story.

Author's Note

The Elemental Kingdom Dark and Light

The elemental kingdom is vast, much as the animal kingdom or plant kingdom is here on Earth. Only bigger. 'Elemental' is a generic word for everything non-human or animal, spirit or otherwise. It covers everything, ranging from the demonic beings in the underworld to the mythical creatures we all know about, such as dragons, fairies, pixies, satyrs and suchlike. And it goes all the way to the most basic forms of energy, which are barely sentient but which exist nevertheless, much like the amoeba and similar. They vary in intelligence and personality, just as people do. They are all different.

Believing that elementals exist is not such a massive stretch of the imagination. If you accept there is light then it stands to reason there must be dark. If you accept there are light beings then there must also be dark beings. We are in a contrasting universe: matter and antimatter, light and dark, protons and electrons, yin and yang. Without this contrast we would stagnate and atrophy. Creativity occurs because of this contrast. So, like it or not, dark and light forces exist throughout the known universe and on this planet. Just because we haven't seen elementals or because they aren't scientifically recorded it does not mean that they don't exist. We can't see oxygen in the air but we know it's there.

We only have generally recognised records of most things for the last few thousand years, but we have been around for much, much longer than that. And that's only what we know. Much has not been recorded officially and has been hidden from the general population. And what about other life on this planet in periods when humans may not have been here?

Modern science has only been around for the last few hundred years. Myths and legends often start off in truth and then over time become myths and legends again. I, for one, believe that elementals exist. It helps, of course, that I deal with them on an almost daily basis. They work and exist alongside us in the spirit realm right here on Earth, co-existing and sharing our beautiful planet much as human and animal spirits do.

To be effective in policing these realms it is useful to work with the dark as well as the light. Who better to deal with a dark being, out on the loose in the light where he should not be, than those of his own dark hierarchy? But it can be a tricky business.

Very few people fully work with both light and dark. It is rare to find beings from both sides working alongside each other. An agreement is needed by both sides of the spiritual hierarchy – a soul contract, if you like – for that role, or else problems will arise. Without this agreement, the best-case scenario is that you would not be able to do anything in that field and would be simply blocked. Or, worse, you'd get yourself into a lot of trouble. With entity attachments and hauntings abounding you could make yourself seriously ill and unhappy, and you could risk being beset by ill fortune.

Working with both sides is not to be trifled with and can be dangerous. A little bit of knowledge can be as dangerous as none, as they say, and dabbling without enough knowledge or spirit support could be catastrophic to your health and well-being. And potentially to those around you too.

Having said that, this rarely presents itself as a problem. The spiritually educated leave what they don't feel happy with well alone, and if you are totally unaware, you are left alone by these beings 99 per cent of the time. They are not interested in you if you are closed, so to speak, to the existence of the spirit realms. The one thing to remember is that we live in the physical realm. They live in the spirit realm. You are in charge of your physical realm and so therefore you carry the ultimate power and control.

The elementals have their own hierarchy and society, just as we do. There are ranks and bosses and underlings, with all levels of creatures of all types imaginable existing and working alongside one another. It all depends on what they are and what their function is.

One of the biggest connections with the elemental kingdom is the land. Being more Earth energy-based elementals work with the land and are intrinsically connected to it. Some are dark and some are light, as with all things in the universe. Just because an elemental works for the dark does not make them evil. Of course they can be, but if they step out of line and break their own laws they will also be pulled up and dealt with, much as in our physical reality. If a person commits a crime, the authorities will track them down, arrest them and deal with them accordingly. It is no different in the dark realms. And at the higher levels there is an accord, an understanding that they will work together.

But, never forget, darkness is darkness. And light is light. It is the nature of darkness to deceive and manipulate. You could arguably tame a lion or a tiger. But still, you would never know if it may just decide to attack you or not. That is, after all, in its nature. It is the same with the dark ones.

If you work with such dark beings you must always be aware

of this. Even with the dark ones who have lawful authority to work for the greater good and who help to maintain the balance alongside the light beings, you need to keep your awareness about you. They will appeal to certain aspects of your character. Ego, for example, is a big one…they will know that you probably have feelings of wanting power. And they often have their own agenda, but mask it with offers of help.

You need to be able to see through this and always be on your guard. It's a risky business. When you do this job you often feel that you are walking along the top of the fence and can be pulled to either side. It's a delicate balance, one that can be hard to maintain.

As I just mentioned, the land has many elemental beings within it. Pixies or fairies could be playing in your garden and larger beings might be close by. The more countrified the area, the more there are. Larger beings will be in charge of certain land areas, supervising and keeping things in order. They will be looking after the land, ensuring its well-being with good energy and healthy plants, water and animals.

In cases where people are often sick and unhappy, where they are suffering from misfortune, where residential disputes are occurring, and where contracts and building developments are falling through and suchlike, often it can be due to sickness in the land. It's the job of the elemental kingdom, of those in lawful authority, to look after the land and keep it positive.

These beings could be anything. But one of the most prominent elementals in charge of land such as parks and common land is the satyr. These wonderful beings come in varying sizes and appearances but generally are half-goat, half-humanoid. The ones I have worked with most frequently are these, and typically have a goat's legs with a humanoid body and two horns on their head, which is sometimes humanoid, sometimes not. And there are Earth elementals, rock elementals, air, fire and water elementals also. Other elementals will have other roles to play. Much as a large corporate body has different roles for different people, so it is within the elemental kingdom.

There will be beings of higher rank governing larger pieces of land. If you cast your mind back to your history lessons, to the days of dukes, barons, earls, peasants, soldiers and knights in shining armour in charge of the land, it is comparable to that. There are divas and deities and other elementals that have no name to you and me. And, like all factions, there are boundaries and opposing groups and individuals: those who rightfully govern an area and those who do not and who wish to usurp them. They attempt to take control of the land and its associated beings for themselves. Battles and wars occur. Just like with humans.

CHAPTER 1

THE COUP

Some years ago Mark had started working closely with a local pet crematorium in southern England. The owner, a caring, spiritual man called Gary, was a regular client of Mark's and had come to see him for some healing one morning, for his usual maintenance.

Mark had an inkling that something was amiss as soon as Gary arrived. As he sat upstairs in the study, patiently waiting, he heard a car pulling onto his drive. Glancing out of the window, he saw his client's black BMW estate come to a halt outside. Seconds later Gary climbed out of his car and immediately Mark could see a nasty elemental clinging to his back, feeding off his light. It appeared as a dark shadow-like being with four appendages, a body and a head, but none of it particularly distinct.

When you look at an elemental it's not like seeing physical things with our physical eyes. It is totally different. It's like viewing things in your peripheral vision or looking at an X-ray. Sometimes, if you are lucky or the entity does not hide, you get a clearer view in greater detail. The more advanced and connected you become, the clearer you 'see'. But everyone 'sees' in a different way.

With alarm bells ringing, Mark swiftly descended the stairs. His defences slammed into place as he closed himself down and grounded himself. His shields were up and he was focusing on his inner light and strength. Standing in his power, Mark was prepared for battle if needed.

No sooner had Gary walked through the front door than Mark stopped him.

'Hi, Gary. Stop here a minute, please. I need to take something off you now.'

Hearing the commanding tone in his voice, and because he was very familiar with Mark's supernatural abilities, Gary stood where he was, trusting him completely.

Mark's guide immediately came forward. Working through him, Mark went straight to Gary's back. Taking a firm grip at the base of his spine and neck, he lifted the dark elemental clear of his energy fields, where it had been locked in around Gary's spine.

Once he had passed the hapless being over to the appropriate forces it was taken away. After taking a careful look about his energy fields it was then that the powers that be chose to speak to him.

'There is a coup happening at the pet crematorium.' Of course Mark knew exactly where they meant. 'The rightful elemental forces in charge have been usurped and a new and powerful dark elemental has taken control of the land without permission. We want you to go there.'

Scenes appeared in his mind's eye, particularly of one couple, who were being psychically attacked by dark beings while they walked around the crematorium grounds. The beings were latching onto their auras and sucking their life force like energy vampires.

Animal souls of all types were being terrorised by the new regime now in charge. Rabbits, cats, dogs, birds, and all sorts of pets were trapped and terrified. Many were cowering in the corners of the kiln areas, unable to cross over and in a state of mass fear.

The new elemental in charge was ruling with fear and terror. Any of the animals that didn't comply were brutally disposed of or maimed, and this was having a knock-on effect in the physical world. The animal kingdom, far more in tune with nature and energies, was suffering too, and many of the animals had deserted the area.

Three main elementals were brought before Mark's eyes. One of them, large and powerful, was clearly in command. Two lesser beings, lieutenants, who were only slightly smaller, served under him. Their minions roamed the grounds.

Knowing that Gary was open to all aspects of his work, Mark questioned him to glean any indicators that things felt different there, or not right. After hearing what Mark had just been told himself, Gary listened and paused thoughtfully.

'It has felt a little different recently. I had noticed, but didn't put two and two together. Do you want to come over?'

'Yes. I've been told that I need to. There is something going on over there and it needs to be sorted.'

An hour later Gary left, and arrangements were made for Mark to visit the pet crematorium the following week. Interestingly, he'd had the urge to visit there for the last month. Now he knew why. Helping out with releasing any animal spirits that may be lost or trapped, clearing the land, and generally keeping the energetic realms in a positive space there was a job he'd already done a few times for Gary.

Obviously events had accelerated somewhat and action could not be delayed.

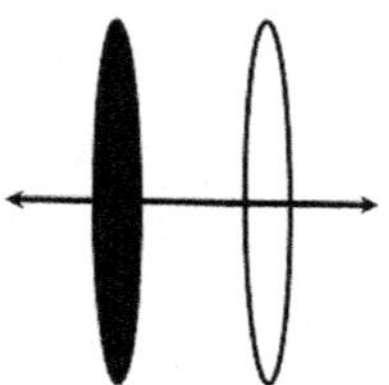

Chapter 2

Gosh Cat

That evening Mark was sitting having dinner in the lounge when he sensed the presence of Gosh, his old cat who had passed over to spirit a couple of years before. Gosh was now an animal spirit guide who worked at the pet crematorium sometimes, helping the other animal spirits cross over. In physical life Gosh had been an amazing cat with an incredible personality. Most people who saw him declared that he acted more like a human than a cat – an old soul, so to speak. In spirit form he had become very much wiser and more knowing.

As soon as he appeared next to him by the door, looking scared and wild-eyed, Mark knew instantly that something was very wrong. Gosh jumped on to a spare chair by his side and slumped down. Distressed and clearly in pain, he laid his head on the seat.

Looking down, Mark saw what appeared to be talon marks running along the cat's flanks. Running deep, with blood seeping between ripped flaps of skin, they were horrific. Something had viciously attacked him with murderous intent. Mark mouthed 'My God', under his breath, then placed his hands either side of Gosh, who started to glow white. Mark channelled healing energy directly over his wounds and through his entire being, easing the pain and repairing the wounds. As light continued to surround Gosh the talon marks slowly closed, eventually leaving no visible trace that they had ever been there.

Moments later Gosh sagged, and an audible sigh could be heard from him. The most he would give away was that he was suffering, but clearly grateful.

Speaking to him in his mind, Mark asked him,

'What happened?'

Slowly Gosh answered and recounted the events. Rather than direct words, it was more a sense of what he wished to convey. But, in truth, there was very little difference between that and speech, except that this was much faster and more accurate.

He had been at the pet crematorium, on his usual patrol, when out of nowhere dark forces had attacked the grounds. Totally unprepared, they had swept aside all defences. The powerful dark elemental lord who commanded the attack had overthrown the elemental in charge. The rightful lord and his forces, caught completely by surprise, were easily defeated and swiftly disappeared. It was over in minutes.

The usurper and his forces now had complete control and occupied the immediate area up to the crematorium boundaries. Everyone was living in terror under the occupying force, which was ruling with cruelty and fear as its weapons. Some of the animals had managed to flee. Others were in hiding or just cowering under the new rule of terror.

Seeing the dark attack, Gosh had reacted with speed. Knowing the battle was already lost and the situation dire, he had to warn someone. He managed to escape during the confusion, and had only just managed to get past the guards to come and inform Mark. Hence the talon marks. Had he been caught he would have been killed. Or worse, tortured, and killed later.

As the narration of the events unfolded, the reality of what happened sank in and Mark felt his emotions rise. Pain, sorrow and grief at Gosh's injuries slowly transformed into rage. He could feel it welling up inside him, building until he was almost totally consumed.

If there is one thing he wouldn't tolerate it was the ones he loved and cared about being hurt intentionally by another.

Consumed with rage, Mark's eyes blazed as he raised his head and arms to the heavens and screamed out his fury for all in the spirit realm, both light and dark, to hear.

Gathering his thoughts moments later, he spoke out to the universe in deadly tones.

'Tell him. Tell him I am coming for him and his time there is finished. I will wreak havoc and rain fiery hell and destruction on this being for what he has done. He will not survive, and death awaits.'

He sensed the message reach across the spirit realms to the dark lord usurper…and it heard him.

After a few days of healing and convalescing, Mark deemed Gosh was fit enough to leave if he wished. But he stayed mostly at Mark's house, where it was safe. Occasionally he made forays out, Mark knew not where, but always he returned. By the time Thursday came round a calmness and a resolution had descended upon Mark. Vengeance and justice was in his heart.

However, the stark reality was that he had to obey the universal rules. Mark's power had been granted based on this fact and begrudgingly he accepted this. But he had no doubt that a battle was coming, and he would do what he had to do. And if that meant destroying this being, then so be it.

Deep down Mark knew that he might be given no choice but to hand the usurper over to the authorities after the battle, for them to deal with themselves.

Author's Note

It should be noted at this time that spirit can talk to us in many ways. Some 'hear' the messages and conversation from spirit: clairaudience. Others 'see' their messages: clairvoyance.

One person I knew described it as like a film being played in front of his eyes. Others 'see' it in different ways. Some 'sense' the messages or information being given: clairsentience. And others have a 'knowing' of what is being told to them: claircognisance. Again, this varies from person to person, depending on their abilities and who they are communicating with. These are commonly called the four 'clairs'.

There are other ways in which spirit can communicate with you, of course, but that is generally how a medium will connect. Or you can have a combination of two or more abilities.

Mark possessed this combination of abilities, and used all four methods combined to some degree all the time.

Chapter 3

The Battle

After deciding to wait and see how it all played out, Mark drove over to the crematorium and let Gary know he was there. He knew the general plan of events, and they walked around the grounds a little first so Mark could get a feel for what was going on.

As soon as he had pointed out where he had seen the couple being attacked the week before in his vision, Gary confirmed that he had seen a couple in that exact place and they had looked very uncomfortable. Much more than he expected for people grieving over the loss of their pet. It had somehow been different.

Gary walked back towards the office, leaving Mark to continue walking around the grounds on his own.

There were two kilns. An old tilting one, dating back a hundred and fifty years, and a new one, built in the last decade or so. The new one was situated close to the entrance and furthest from the grounds. The old one was further in and situated right next to the main open garden. Previously used for smelting metal when originally constructed in the early 1900s, the kiln had been adapted for use in the late 1990s for its current purpose.

Approaching the kiln, he felt uncomfortable and paused to observe it. There was definitely an issue there but deciding it could wait till later he moved on.

The main central garden, usually a peaceful area, had a small tree in the centre, laden abundantly with pink blossom. A couple of bird feeders hung among its branches, and a bird table, with similar feeders, stood away from the reach of the tree's canopy. Usually bustling with activity, it was eerily quiet in the obvious absence of any birds. Nor were there any animal spirits. Most days they could be seen wandering around, happy to stay in this tranquil place.

Once Mark had moved back into the more cultivated section on the border of the grounds he stopped again. Motionless, focusing his attention and taking stock of everything around him in his mind's eye, he stood thus for some twenty minutes.

Gradually a sense of the scene appeared in his mind and a picture materialised of the occupying enemy forces dotted about the grounds. They were in no set formation, but rather in groups gathered at strategic locations. Other detachments patrolled the area. It was clear that some form of martial law had been imposed, because everyone was in hiding. A dark cloud covered the grounds like a giant canopy.

Unbidden, sensing the battle to come, the deposed light elementals started appearing around and behind him. After asking for both light and dark forces to come to his aid, they appeared, joining ranks with the rightful beings waiting to deal with the invaders.

The mood was grim and determined as Mark slowly walked forward. His own mood reflected that of those he stood with, his mouth held in a tight line with pent-up anger. Spirit and elemental reinforcements formed a mass behind him and flanked him on either side in a long line. Numbering in their hundreds, they continued to appear from all directions. Resolute in regaining their rightful land, vengeance was strong in their minds, and they strained against invisible leashes, eager to engage the enemy.

Moments later the line rolled forward, like an unstoppable force of nature, covering the ground as far as the eye could see, both physically and spiritually.

The dark forces of the usurper moved out to oppose them. Both forces stopped. For a moment they glared at each other. Then, picking up pace, the lines swept forward. Mark's forces swept past the usurper, eagerly seeking combat. Crackling energy filled the air about him as moments later the two forces clashed. The shock waves reverberated across the crematorium grounds.

Violence was everywhere as beings on both sides were either taken away or sometimes just vanishing. Silent screams rent the air and the atmosphere cracked and hummed with static electricity, making Mark's hair stand on end. The fighting was fierce, with no quarter given on either side. The raging battle ebbed and flowed, but inexorably Mark's forces slowly drove the usurpers back.

For a moment he paused. With the experience of a natural-born leader and warrior Mark surveyed the carnage about him. Then he walked over to the garden area with the small blossom tree and saw a large dark elemental, clearly one of rank.

As they looked at each other he realised it was one of the two lieutenants, who was joint second in command with his counterpart. Mark's anger rose at the sight of one of the beings responsible for the injuries inflicted on Gosh. He gathered his strength and swiftly moved over to him.

A huge elemental light warrior named Ralok, one who Mark had worked with before, stepped into him and took control, using his body as a vessel. An immediate sense of invincibility and power flowed through Mark's being. With a silent roar Ralok/Mark reached forward and took hold of the lieutenant in a vice-like grip, with one hand tight around its throat and the other hooked into its abdomen.

A dark portal, subconsciously summoned by Mark and his guides, opened up just to the side. For a few short moments a battle of will and strength ensued before the lieutenant was hoisted off the ground, its feet kicking frantically in the air. It was helpless. Swinging round, the Ralok/Mark hybrid dangled the hapless lieutenant over the portal. The dark powers that governed it could be seen waiting by the entrance. With a mighty shove Mark propelled it into waiting arms, which dragged it down to the depths below. The portal closed instantly.

Sensing movement behind, Mark spun around and was suddenly confronted by the second lieutenant. Outstretched claw-like hands reached for his throat and jet-black eyes gleamed in triumph.

Quick as lightning Mark's hand flashed out, taking hold of it by what was as close to a throat as you could picture. The other hand dug deeply into its centre mass.

Stopped dead in its tracks, the lieutenant screamed in rage and frustration as its claws strived to reach Mark's throat. Only vaguely humanoid in shape, more a shifting dark mass, the being squirmed in his grip as it frantically tried to fight back. Mark viciously twisted his hands and the second lieutenant grunted in pain. With his rage barely in check, Mark's hands dug ever deeper into its core energy, streaming burning white light through them both. Screaming in new-found agony, the realisation sank in that it was losing, and triumph and rage turned to fear as its struggles became frantic in an effort to escape rather than attack. But it had no chance. None at all.

Another portal materialised on the ground next to the lieutenant. Ralok/Mark stomped over to its open maw and shoved it forcefully into the inky depths and the waiting hierarchy of the underworld.

While taking a second to breathe, Mark surveyed the field of combating forces. The battle raged across the grounds as he studied the second kiln. More like an old chimney, which in fact it was, the building looked archaic.

The brickwork was off-centre and the entire structure had a slight lean to it. Approximately fifty feet high and circular in shape, it narrowed as it rose to the top, where an opening could be seen with heat rising above. Some feet below the top spire a ledge, wide enough for someone to stand on, extended around the entire circumference. The enemy elementals were camped on it, like on the parapet of a castle, and throwing objects down on his forces.

With a gesture, and with orders to some of his commanding officers, Mark directed them to take the ledge. Moments later, light forces streamed up the chimney walls to engage the enemy.

Mark stepped forward and a beam of energy shot from his upraised hand, blasting an elemental off the ledge, which tumbled to the ground below. Three more followed suit and then his own force was there among them, viciously fighting hand to hand, slashing and grappling for supremacy of this strategic location. The fighting was fierce, but several minutes later the ledge was clear. The dark invaders were either disposed of or captured.

While walking across the grass he sensed something evil and steered himself towards a wooded area on the boundaries of the crematorium. A gated entrance appeared ahead.

Striding towards it he saw the gate was bolted but the padlock unlocked. After sliding the bar across he pushed open the metal gate and walked in to survey the grounds. Not quite as neat as the main footpath but still well kept, a path of wood chippings meandered to the left.

Above the path was a slope of mixed grass and earth with many small pet gravestones and markers along its sides. A small stairway had been cut into its side with single paving slabs on each step to facilitate reaching the summit. Twenty metres up, the slope came to an abrupt stop. Beyond was a forest. A fence with two metal wires between posts lined the boundary, marking the edge of the forest and the end of the crematorium grounds.

Mark paused and looked up at the forest. The energy was ominous in feel, and instinctively he knew something was up there.

Without warning a long line of dark elementals appeared, rising up from behind the summit and the hidden gully behind. As he looked from side to side he sensed the dark forces opposite staring at him maliciously, feeling his perceived vulnerability while he was on his own, and savouring the moment before they attacked.

Mark stood there, staring back impassively. Raising his arms, light beings appeared as if from nowhere at his side, of an equal number to those who opposed him.

'Well?' he said out loud, with a challenging note in his voice.

He sensed the confidence of the dark elementals waver. His mood was still grim and he was in no mood to play gently. Unbidden, his energy merged with the light beings alongside him. His power gathered, building till he could contain no more, or else he would explode.

Mark's arms spread wide and white light radiated out in a line of pure force, with him at the centre opposite the dark ones. His arms swept forward and the force of light swept with them, smashing into the dark ranks with a silent thunderclap of crashing energy and disintegrating them on impact. Moments later the white light vanished as quickly as it had appeared, and waves of hot aftermath energy rose up where the opposing line had once stood.

An eerie stillness could be felt and Mark walked up the rough paved steps to the top of the summit and looked intently into the forest.

Seconds later a dark form appeared between the trees some thirty metres ahead.

Tall and broad, he recognised it as being the one in charge of this forest. Though it had not directly ordered the attack, it nevertheless was in overall command and could not be allowed to stay. Being so close to the crematorium, the forest was of strategic importance, and would be used as a staging point for further attacks on the grounds.

'You cannot stay here,' Mark called out loud. 'It is time for you to leave.'

Assessing him, the dark form looked at him. Mark could feel it was deciding what to do. It didn't want to give up its position. But, having just witnessed such a display of raw power and the ease with which Mark had disposed of its forces, crushing them totally, it was uncertain about what to do.

Taking advantage of its hesitation Mark's hands rose, and a burst of intense white light shot out and smote the dark form full in the centre of its chest. The light penetrated deep inside and the entry point glowed bright white from within. A look of shock registered on its face before it simply vanished. A stillness hung in the air as, with its passing, the energy of the land shifted.

Mark called out, and a ranking light elemental appeared at the forest edge. Knowing it was here to take over the land, he silently acknowledged it. An unsaid request for assistance came from the light elemental to help him clear up the rest of the forest. With a wave of his hand other light elementals appeared alongside. There was a pause.

'More?' he silently asked. Feeling its answer, Mark gestured again, and yet more light elementals appeared. Dozens now stood alongside the new governing elemental, raising the light force above him to a substantial number.

An unsaid acknowledgement came across, and Mark nodded in satisfaction. The forest was in good hands and they would finish the job of protecting the crematorium borders, and would restore the energy to that of light.

He turned and walked back to the metal gate, then slid the bolt in place as he left the forest behind him. Sensing he was needed, he strode back towards the kiln.

Author's Note

Spirit beings

Throughout this book you will often see different references to various spiritual beings. In particular, soldiers, soldier guides or spirit guides are referred to. This is because they all have different roles. Some can multitask, but at other times you need something more specific.

For example, your general practitioner can do many things, but to find out more about, say, a shoulder injury or a more specific illness, he or she may well refer you to a specialist in that field. Another example would be to compare a regular infantryman to an elite special forces soldier from the SAS, or an explosives expert. It is the same within the spirit world. A spirit guide can guide you and help you in a number of ways. But, for example, if you were fighting another spiritual being of an unusual nature or a very powerful one you may need to use a spirit being more suited to that task. A soldier or a warrior. The right tool for the right job.

The more powerful you are, the higher the level of spiritual beings you are likely to work with, and greater numbers of them. It's like comparing a large corporate company to the local corner shop. This also relates, of course, to the role you play in the grand scheme of things. A great medium, for example, would not need as many beings. He or she does one thing. It would be the same with a healer, who may need a few more beings or just work with the one.

Mark, for example, has entire teams behind him and access to many different beings of all levels and power from all different realms (many of which he doesn't even know about till they appear). But he has access to them. He has, as you have witnessed, already summoned a small army.

It's all about your role within the grand scheme of things. If you are meant to fulfil that role you will be given the tools for the job. This is why it is so important to fulfil your role but not overstep your boundaries. You will not get the support if you do.

Many people do overstep their abilities and it never ends well, for you, for the client, or for the spirit world, particularly when it comes to dealing with moving spirit forms on. It's OK for most connected people to move on, say, a spirit of the type of Casper the friendly ghost. Just ask them to leave, and it's likely that they will.

But imagine saying you can help someone with their haunted house. You've listened to what they have said and decided you can help. Then you get to the house and find out that you're dealing with a fully fledged demon lord, or a screaming banshee, or some other equally unsavoury situation. That would be very dangerous for all concerned. If you get involved it's highly likely to make the situation worse and cause more problems for the client and the person who said they could deal with it. Ill health, bad fortune, mental and emotional trauma could result, just to begin with, for both parties. And the entity is still there, potentially now aggravated and angry.

So it's important to recognise something which is not within your life contract or abilities to deal with. As soon as you get that feeling, walk away. Recommend that they find another person to deal with it, and, if you're able, point them in the direction of someone who can. It's all about the right person for the right job. There are always more clients.

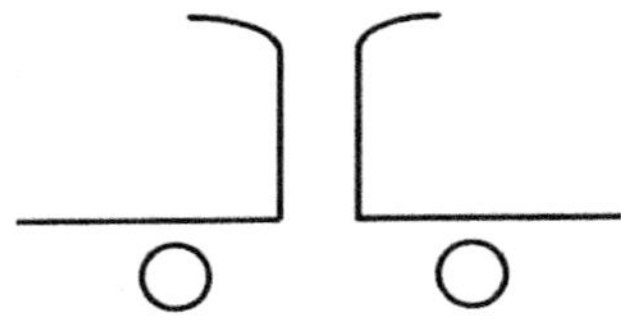

Chapter 4

Dark Lord Usurper

While moving to the other side of the kiln Mark sensed the dark elemental lord that had taken control of the crematorium. His guides and guards moved closer to be next to him.

Ralok, who had now vacated Mark's body, stood highest among them. The usurper made its presence known and appeared directly in front of him. Seven feet in height and larger than the other two, it approached. Its body seemingly flowed and moved in such a way that made it hard for the eye to pick out detail. Menacing and confident, it moved towards Mark.

Sensing a disturbance in the Earth energies behind him, Mark briefly cast an eye towards his right. The demon lord he worked with rose up from the earth behind him, materialising through a portal of its own making. Huge and grotesque, with power and authority emanating from it, it glowered at the usurper. Other light forces were close by also, ready to be there at a moment's notice.

The dark elemental lord stopped its advance and stood a few metres in front of him. Its body settled, allowing it to be visible in greater detail. Roughly humanoid in shape and undoubtedly male, its exact features were still indistinguishable. Its body was dark, and had a course and leathery almost bark like skin, with two long powerful arms and legs. A large angular head sat on top of its narrow neck. Two beady red eyes looked Mark up and down, getting the measure of him.

Holding its gaze, Mark glanced around him, surveying the scene. The tide of battle had turned in Mark's favour and it knew it. Returning his gaze, he looked at the creature ultimately responsible for the injuries to Gosh and felt his rage-filled emotions shift to ones of resoluteness and justice. With his spirit voice he spoke.

'Well? What's it to be? Your forces are defeated and you have lost. Your time here is done.'

For several long moments the dark lord just looked at Mark and locked eyes with him. Then its eyes flicked over the forces with Mark. The balance of power had turned.

A black portal opened next to it, beckoning. Either way, it would be going into that portal. It knew it. Mark knew it.

Its red eyes gazed again over the force in front of him and the remnants of its own forces within the battlefield. It had lost. Casting a last glance at Mark and without a word, it stepped into the inky depths of the underworld and vanished.

Stepping back Mark took a deep breath. With the dark commanders gone the battle was all but won. Now was just a case of mopping up the remnants, sending them to their correct realms and re-establishing the rightful governors of this land.

As he walked around the grounds Mark supervised the clearing up. Small pockets of resistance and stragglers were overcome with relative ease. Taking a direct hand where needed, he took stock of the aftermath and the energy residue. It was dark. A battle like this compounded the negativity, leaving a stain on the land unless dealt with.

Calling the light forces together, combining their power, and drawing light from the skies above, he walked around the grounds in a long line, cleansing and clearing away all the negativity. It took an hour of hard labour and was exhausting.

On completion, he took stock of his work. Although tired and drained, a sense of satisfaction ensued as he surveyed the scene, noting the improved energy of the land. Not yet as it was before the coup, it was nevertheless much improved.

These things take time. The worst cases can take years for everything to return to normal. Plant life starts to grow again and animals return only once the positive energy returns. However, this was not one of those times and in a matter of weeks, a month or two at the outside, it would be back to normal.

As he strolled over towards the owner to provide a synopsis of the morning's events, Mark walked past the small blossom tree. Stopping for a moment, he watched as birds seemed to fly from all directions, settling on the tree and around it. All over the ground and flying about the crematorium, eating from the bird stands and feeders and chirping their songs, they were everywhere. Always a haven for birds, and an apparent meeting spot, it was busier than he had ever seen it before.

A great feeling of love and rightness came over him. The birds were back. All was as it should be, and justice had been served.

But what would be next? Darkness was coming. They would attack again.

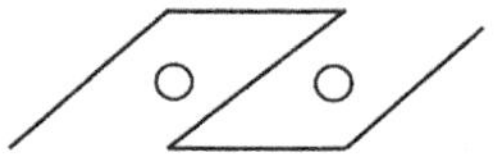

CHAPTER 5

AUSTRALIA

Two weeks later Mark received a call from Stephen Dawson, a colleague in Australia. He explained that there had been weird goings-on at a shopping mall close to him. Just outside Sydney, the mall had been built only a decade or so ago. But there was significant history related to the site before its construction. Previously the land had been used as an industrial estate but all the businesses had failed for one reason or another, and had gone into liquidation then closure. The shutting down of the failed industrial estate had led to a redevelopment of the site, and the idea of the shopping mall was conceived. Prior to that the land had been mainly brush and desert, but owned and inhabited by aborigines native to the land for centuries.

Stephen was also a healer and was very good at tuning into the energies of the land and sensing energies around him. He continued to relate what he had heard to Mark. After hearing some stories in the news of financial upsets within the community, of businesses struggling, and even accounts of frayed tempers and scuffles breaking out, he had investigated.

A pattern of unrest was forming. His investigations revealed that the resident aborigines had claimed that there were ancient burial grounds, unmarked but present on the site, which should not be disturbed. No one knew exactly how long they had been there but the land was purported to be holy ground. As there was no actual proof of these claims, they were swept aside by big corporations and their lawyers, who had offered to pay money in compensation and to rehouse the aborigines in another area. And that is exactly what happened. The development of the mall went ahead regardless.

On attending the mall Stephen had looked around and discovered some areas with an alarming negative energy to them. In the main food court area, particularly, he sensed a very strong vibe of hostility permeating the vicinity, washing over everyone and everything. Knowing there was a fair chance he would be detected as a sensitive and therefore more vulnerable to attack, he had quickly left and called Mark later that day.

After putting the phone down Mark mulled over what he had been told. He trusted Stephen and knew he wasn't prone to exaggerating. Having listened to his narration of events, he knew something serious was likely to have happened and he needed to investigate. With his mind made up, Mark logged on to his PC and booked his flight over to Sydney for the following week.

Author's Note

It is worth noting that communication with spirit beings takes many forms. This also varies depending on who the communicator is. We can work in different ways. However, as often as not it is more in the form of 'knowing' or 'feeling' what they are trying to communicate, or a combination of both. This is particularly true when connecting to non-human beings such as demons or elementals.

Chapter 6

Kuala Lumpur

One week later Mark was sitting in the airport, waiting to board his flight. Despite the long journey he was looking forward to the trip, and had decided to break it up a little by making a stopover in Kuala Lumpur for three nights. This was roughly midway and he hadn't visited that city before, so it was a good opportunity to visit a new country and experience the culture, the people and the energy of the land.

It wasn't long before his flight appeared on the information screen, asking him to proceed to his gate for boarding. After boarding the plane he settled into his seat and prepared for take-off. Although he was usually happy with flying, a feeling of unease came over him as they approached the runway. Digging into his feelings, he tried to analyse the source of his discomfort. But no sooner had he done so when the feeling vanished.

Mark took a deep breath and slowly exhaled, allowing the tension to flow out of him. Something was amiss, he knew. When, where and what were an entirely different matter. Resigning himself to the fact there there was nothing he could do about it for now, he let it go.

The plane took off without mishap. He settled down into his seat and immediately closed his eyes to rest.

The journey finished and Mark's plane landed with a jolt. It had been a relatively smooth ride but the landing had marred the journey somewhat. Mark frowned. Still, he had arrived in one piece, he said to himself, so was grateful for that.

He disembarked and made his way through customs after collecting his luggage. Then he was met by his pre-booked driver and almost immediately found himself arriving at his hotel. After being escorted to reception he was shown to his room, and his luggage was dropped off by the porter a few minutes later.

Mark looked out of the large window, which extended from wall to wall and from floor to ceiling. He was seventeen floors up and the view was spectacular. In front of the hotel was a beautiful, partly sculpted park.

Kuala Lumpur was built on what had originally been a jungle, and the park reflected that. Magnificent-looking trees were dotted around, with several meandering pathways. Small architectural structures and seating areas under cover were conveniently situated around the grounds for people to relax and enjoy the ambience. Small knolls were artfully scattered about the park area, which rose up and down in gentle curves and dips, with unusual-looking trees set in groups around the knolls and other strategic places. Idly he wondered what kind of trees they were. The trunks seemed to be made of many small trunks all winding upwards together with a large canopy spread above.

Far off to one side he could see a small man-made lake that had a beautiful water feature in the shape of a whale, with water fountains that spewed patterns high into the air.

The park was the centrepiece to an area surrounded by buildings on the outskirts with walkways dividing the two. Restaurants ringed two sides and business centres and high-rise buildings another. The famous Petronas Twin Towers stood majestically with amazing detailed architecture and a glass-floored bridge that spanned the area between them halfway up. A huge shopping mall was on another side and a brick-paved path went all the way around the outside of the park for people to walk on, sharing it with small open electric shuttles taking people from one place to the next.

Shrugging off his jet lag, Mark had a shower, put on some cool clothes and made his way downstairs to the front of the hotel.

As he stepped onto the path he dipped into the atmosphere. As was typical in an Asian country, it was hot and a little humid but not unpleasant, a nice change from the chilly weather he had just left behind in England. Dressed in a lightweight T-shirt and jeans, he let out a sigh of pleasure and walked over to the park edge towards a wooden bench overlooking the grounds, which he felt would be good to meditate on and tune into the land. Aiming to offset his jet lag and ground himself he sat down, made himself comfortable, and closed his eyes.

While taking a few deep breaths and feeling his feet on the lush grass he grounded, sending his roots deep down, bringing his breath into a deep slow rhythm, and relaxing his entire body as he did so.

As he settled into a deep meditative state his meditation was disturbed. His ever-aware senses picked up something untoward. Something big and non-human was approaching him in front from the park.

Instantly he opened his eyes and his shields slammed down into place, closing him down as he entered a state of high awareness. Looking in front across the park, some thirty metres away stood a huge Earth elemental, roughly three metres high. Vaguely humanoid in shape and with a dense body it stood there, making no move to approach him further. As he extended his senses he felt the energy and realised it wasn't a threat. But the entire atmosphere in the park seemed to have changed and was no longer peaceful.

Using his spirit voice Mark spoke with his mind.

'What do you want?' he asked.

Communicating as much in feelings and images the Earth elemental answered,

'We have been overthrown and need your help. A dark force has taken over our land and we have been brought down. We are no longer in control and we need you.'

Silently it stood there, waiting for an answer but somehow still communicating the same message.

Staying where he was on the bench, Mark remained motionless, absorbing the information. For a moment he raised his mind to the universe while mouthing the thought,

'Why me?'

But he knew why. It was his job and life path. Instantly he dismissed the thought and set his mind to the task. Communicating his acquiescence without words, the Earth elemental silently acknowledged him and moved back out of sight, and Mark dismissed its energy from his thoughts.

Closing his eyes again he extended his senses further out, taking in the energy of the park and feeling for anything dark or negative. He wasn't long in finding it.

Projecting his spirit form out of his body he travelled around the park. And now he could see the energy was sick. Everywhere he saw dark forms dipping in and out of sight as he travelled, ducking behind trees and structures as he passed. Mark's energy intensified and shone brighter, seeking the source, and became a shining beacon among the surrounding dark energy.

Every now and then small dark elementals would stay in sight for a little too long. Reaching out, Mark would grab the hapless victims and toss them into the waiting hands of the light beings he knew were around him. But, knowing they would do their job, he paid little attention to them.

Mentally calling out, he challenged the source of this dark overtaking.

'I'm coming for you. I challenge your authority for this land. Come out and show yourself.'

A roar answered and a huge dark being appeared from behind a copse of trees at the top of a knoll in front of him.

With his shields in place Mark braced himself, solidifying his energies and gathering his strength.

Vaguely humanoid, with blurred energy when looked at directly, Mark could feel and sense it as much as see it. Dark energies rolled off it in waves as it roared in rage at Mark's challenge.

Working itself up into a frenzy, it edged towards him, and then, extending its long arms, it charged. Instantly a white light shield appeared in front of Mark. The dark elemental slammed into it with a silent crash and was thrown back several metres by the impact. Stunned and surprised, it roared its anger at the invisible force that blocked it from its intended victim.

As it rushed back at Mark the elemental was stopped dead in its tracks again. Frustration and rage were etched on its features as it tried to break through, hammering futilely against the shield.

Beams of bright white light streamed from Mark's hands and slammed into its body. Knocked back, the elemental staggered. The beams of light changed to ones of containment, and wrapped around its throat and middle core energy. Mark tightened his grip as the elemental, held fast, screamed in impotent rage. A dark portal opened up in the ground alongside it and a demon lord stepped out. Large and powerful, it worked for the higher authority within the dark realms.

Mark spoke out loud to the usurper.

'Your time is up and you will go back to whence you came.'

The demon lord grasped the dark elemental with taloned hands bigger and stronger than its own. Mark's light beams stayed locked around it and pushed it towards the waiting portal while the demon lord dragged it with him. After stepping over the portal they both dropped down out of sight and the portal closed behind them.

Mark released his bonds and took stock of the situation. Feeling out, he moved around the park, and let everything know that the uprising was over. The lesser dark entities started to disappear as though answering some silent summons. The lawful light elementals appeared and streamed over the land, mopping up any dark entities left, and reclaimed their park.

Mark brought himself back to his physical body and saw the lawful Earth elemental appear in front of him again.

'Thank you,' it said with gratitude.

'You are welcome,' Mark silently replied.

With that the Earth elemental moved off to retake his park and commence the healing process of the land.

Mark took a deep breath and settled into himself. It was draining to do that kind of work, to step out of your physical body and fight in spirit form. It soaked up your inner energy, which you also felt physically. It was like having a long, hard fight in the physical world.

'So much for the easy three-day stopover,' he said to himself with a wry smile.

Standing up he moved off to walk through the park in physical form. As he walked along the meandering pathway, feeling the energy as he did so, he could feel it shifting and gradually becoming lighter. His work here was finished.

Deciding he deserved a well-earned break, he found a quiet coffee house overlooking the park and sat down.

Pleased with himself and the work he had done, yet again he was reminded of the greater good and his role. It was not all about paying clients, as so many people thought. But he embraced this role and took satisfaction in the fact that he was here to help. Which, of course, was no accident. It had all been 'arranged'.

On thinking things through, he considered that this could be the work of Archdemon Belthazar.** But Michael had forced his retreat at their last encounter.

Had he returned? If not, then who else? Some other high dark power? Either way, dark forces were boldly showing their hand in different places around the world. It was another sign that things were escalating.

Well, one thing was for sure, he thought. This trip certainly wasn't going to be uneventful.

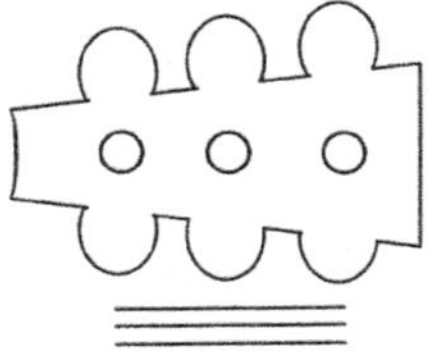

** Story recited in Book 1. The Diary of a Gatekeeper.

Chapter 7

Sydney

Three days later Mark arrived at Sydney Airport and was greeted by Stephen as he exited the gates.

'Hi, Mark, how's things? It's good to see you,' Stephen said, with genuine pleasure etched on his features.

'Hi, Stephen. Good to see you too. How's the other half? How have you been?' Mark replied.

Stephen took one of his bags and indicated they should walk.

'The car is just in the car park. First level. Let's get going to avoid the rush hour, and we can talk on the way.'

After finding their way to the car park and loading the car, it wasn't long before they were on their way to Stephen's house.

The two friends exchanged small talk for a while, catching up on mundane day-to-day events. Then Stephen paused.

'It's great to have you here, Mark, but I wouldn't have called you unless it was urgent and I really thought you should know. I've been keeping an eye on things, like you wanted me to. I have noticed how things seem to be changing. The energy of the land just seems to be different. People generally are different. And life. Businesses seem to be failing more often, and people are not so friendly. There are more domestic incidents being reported and petty crime seems to be on the rise. Things are just not so good at the moment. It feels wrong somehow,' he said with feeling.

'I know,' replied Mark. 'I feel it too.'

'And when I first went to the mall a few weeks ago and saw what was going on I knew something was wrong there. I went back a second time to double-check. And a third time.'

Mark looked at his old friend. He looked unsettled. Worried. He had known Stephen a long time and had even started his spiritual journey with him many years ago. They had followed different paths ultimately, but he still kept his hand in and was very aware. Some things he could deal with himself, and often did if he felt the need. To have called Mark it must be serious.

'Mark, something is seriously wrong there. I was basically attacked on my last visit. They recognised I was aware and made their presence felt by probing and pushing my energy fields.' He paused and continued.

'It felt like it was in two parts almost. Some sections felt kind of OK. Others not. I sensed a mass of unwelcoming beings in the food hall area. It made me feel very sick and, to be honest, it was a little scary. Too much for me to deal with.'

Mark nodded.

'You know me, Mark. I'm not one to avoid anything, but that was too big. So I left. And decided to call you.'

'You did the right thing, Steve,' Mark said, placing one hand on his friend's shoulder. 'I needed to know, and that's what I'm here for.'

He looked at Stephen carefully and saw the look of slight trepidation on his face.

'What is it? Is there something else I should know?'

Thoughtfully Stephen spoke.

'I'm not sure. I felt there was something else behind this, Mark.

It was hidden from me, but not completely. Something lurking in the background. Something more. Something very dark. I'm telling you, Mark, it scared me. That's when I left.'

With firmness in his voice Mark answered reassuringly.

'Don't worry, my friend, I'll deal with it. We'll get to the bottom of it and find out who, or what, is behind this. Then we'll do what is needed and send them back to where they belong.'

Stephen's energy settled and the rest of the journey passed swiftly.

On arrival at Stephen's house Mark was shown his room, where he dropped off his luggage. After a leisurely shower and change of clothing he felt much refreshed, and lounged around for a while.

That evening he went downstairs for dinner and was introduced again to Stephen's long-term girlfriend, who he knew slightly from their time in England.

The evening and dinner passed uneventfully and Mark retired to his room. After removing his clothes he climbed under the duvet and fell instantly asleep.

Author's Note

Many people, including light workers, mediums and other beings within this field believe that they are protected by their guides and spirit. This is only partly true.

It is true to say that if you have the right connections, the spirit guides and the other beings you work with will protect you on some level. But ultimately it is your job to protect yourself. The responsibility lies with you. Much as a seat belt will protect you from certain injuries if you have an accident while driving your car, the seat belt on its own will not save you from all forms of harm. It is still your responsibility to put the seat belt on, to drive the car safely, and to consider all the other variables. So it is with your personal protection within the spirit realms. The responsibility lies with you. Not them.

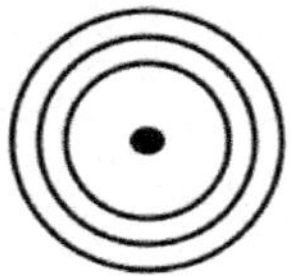

Chapter 8

The Mall

Mark woke the next morning with the sun streaming through his curtains, bathing the room with its warmth. Rolling out of bed he threw on a pair of jeans and T-shirt as well as a pair of his favourite boots. He walked downstairs into the kitchen. Stephen was already there, preparing breakfast.

'Want some?' Stephen asked with a wide grin.

Realising he was ravenous, Mark looked at the sizzling sausages and eggs on the cooker and gladly accepted. After devouring the food they both sat back contentedly and Mark allowed himself to feel peaceful and relaxed. Life was good.

But his thoughts became more sombre as he looked at his friend and the reason for his visit. Turning his attention fully to the task at hand, he spoke up.

'I think we should get straight to it today. How long will it take to get to the mall you're talking about?'

'It's about a thirty-minute drive,' Stephen replied. 'We can leave when you're ready.'

Mark paused and thought for a moment.

'OK, let's go in about fifteen minutes. I just need to get sorted and I'll be ready.'

A quarter of an hour or so later Stephen led them down to the underground garage where his car was kept and they were soon heading out to the mall.

Mark started to prepare, mentally and physically attuning himself so that he was ready.

Within a short space of time they had parked the car and were walking through the main entrance into the mall.

The shopping mall was quite big. Most of it was open, and only a few sections were fully covered. Walkways criss-crossed on the first floor above. Lined with shops, they overlooked the ground floor below and the main areas. The weather there was mostly hot and dry with little rain, so there was not much call for a fully enclosed centre.

Small trees were strategically planted, and a water feature with a fountain spewing water was a central feature in the middle of the mall. Benches were dotted around under the shade of planted trees to provide relaxing places to rest. Footpaths led anywhere and everywhere and the whole centre seemed to be undefined, flowing like a meandering waterway, which, under normal circumstances, would have been good, as it allowed energy to flow better. That and the openness should have given it a familiar, welcoming feel, which is obviously what the architects had intended for the surrounding communities. Not just for shopping, but also somewhere to spend the day.

But not now. To the unaware, everything seemed as it appeared on the surface. Calm, relaxing, almost beautiful. If you scratched a little deeper, though, the veneer slid away.

Allowing himself to dig that little deeper, Mark tuned into the energies. There was an underlying, unfriendly feeling to this place. It was unwelcoming, and now Mark knew what Stephen had been talking about.

Turning to his friend, he spoke.

'I can feel something wrong now also. You said things have been happening here. Businesses going under and problems with people in the area?'

'Yes,' Stephen replied. 'It's not been good. Many businesses have gone under. New ones have taken their place. But still … and in the surrounding areas things haven't prospered. It's like everything is going wrong for the local communities. But this seems to be central. You can feel it.'

'Yes, you can,' Mark replied. 'Let's sit down and have something to eat. Is there somewhere we can go?'

'Sure. There's the central food mall over that way.'

'Isn't that the one you talked about?' Mark asked.

'Yes, it is.'

'OK, let's go, then.'

They headed over to the food court and found an empty table. The tables were metal and mainly small and round, seating four at a push. The area was covered and had a central counter where food was prepared and served.

Mark looked at the menu and saw that it seemed to be healthy food, and when the young waitress came over they both ordered straight away. Their drinks arrived and Mark sat back. Alert to his surroundings, he sipped his drink and looked around.

Sometimes when you see things of a spiritual nature, it is immediate, appearing right in front of you. At other times you gradually get a sense of things not being right, and you have to look for it. Then, as you become more aware of something amiss, they may show themselves. Spirit forms. Energetic beings. Or you may just see them anyway. Often they hide in the shadows, choosing to do their dark deeds from within. Sometimes they may just jump out straight away and want to fight you or challenge you.

It all depends on the situation and what you're dealing with. Just as it is with a person. Everyone and everything is different. So you must be fluid and ready for all eventualities.

Mark was.

The energy took a turn for the worse and became darker and more unfriendly as he sat there. With his senses heightened he felt something gathering behind him, and his shields immediately dropped into place.

Gathering his core energy in a state of readiness, he turned in his seat and looked. A wide dark energetic mass was starting to take form and coalesce.

As he watched, the mass shifted and moved inside itself, then started to separate, seemingly taking on individual forms. Part of him watched the process with detached interest as the energies took their final state. The other part of him was on full alert.

Now complete individual spirits could be seen. They had the appearance of aborigines, all large and strong powerful beings. Not just regular spirits. A semicircle took shape behind him as he turned in his chair to face them directly. Menacing and hostile, they were not here to greet him with open arms. That much was clear.

He waited for them to make the first move, to see what they wanted.

Tuning in, he opened his senses to communicate with them. Rather than direct words, they communicated what they wanted and how they felt in waves of non-verbal communication, so that Mark could sense and 'know' what they had to say.

These were the powerful beings that represented the ancestors of the original aborigines and the more recently deposed ones from their land. Yes, their land. They believed this was their land and that white people had come and taken over, displacing the natives already living here. Not only that, but this was the site of a sacred burial ground deep below the land that had been there for centuries, undisturbed and respected by the modern aboriginal inhabitants.

White Western man had ignored these facts, as they couldn't be proved to the local government and big corporations involved at the time. Their interest was only greed and money.

Mark sat and looked at them. Their anger was palpable, and they were seething from within. It was aimed now at him, as they saw someone who could see them and, to their minds, someone who represented the enemy.

He could feel that anger gaining momentum, and while in the recesses of his mind he acknowledged their situation and maybe genuine grievance, the danger was very real.

Maybe eight or nine very angry spirits faced him.

Without warning, the ranks rushed forward towards him as one. Mark swiftly raised both hands, and a barrier of pure light formed in front of them and stopped their rush abruptly. Surprise and anger were etched on their features as they struck the impenetrable barrier and realised they had been denied their intended prey.

After calling in high-powered beings from above, they reinforced Mark's barrier and then wrapped it around them. These higher-powered beings had authority and were sympathetic to the situation of the aborigines.

This was not a time for punishment but rather one of discussion and help, if they were willing. Leaving his barrier in place to assist, Mark watched the aboriginal spirits being taken away to have their grievance listened to and to see what could be done to help.

Sitting back, Mark took a breath, glad they had been dealt with now. It had been a close call, as he would not have wished to fight that many. That would have been dangerous and hard. And they had a genuine reason to be angry. He was relieved that they had been taken away to be helped rather than face some other harsher outcome. They may have been in the wrong and caused many problems, but they had a reason to feel aggrieved. It was better to be dealt with that way.

But something still didn't feel right. There was something more.

Author's Note

When dealing with angry or malicious spirits, it is not always a case of just removing them with force. Just like unhappy or problematic people, you have to deal with them in the appropriate manner.

That may just be taking them away. But it could also be talking to them, finding out the problem and resolving it. Or it could be just listening and helping them to understand. Every situation is different. You don't necessarily go in with all guns blazing.

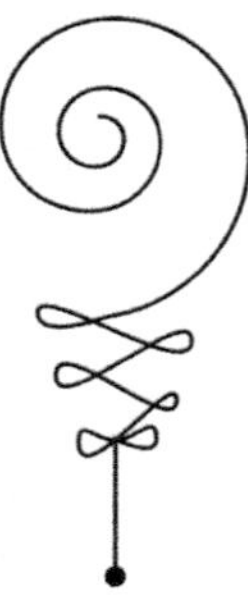

CHAPTER 9

THE CRONE

Stephen sat opposite Mark, watching intently. He could feel something going on, but not exactly what.

Turning to face him, Mark paused a moment then brought him up to speed.

'So they had genuine reason to be upset and angry, then?' Stephen said after he'd finished.

'Yes, they did. But they were very angry and have been causing big problems here. They didn't leave me much room for manoeuvre or time to talk. They formed a semicircle around me after coming out of thin air and attacked me. But I managed to stop them and have them taken away by the higher powers.'

Mark became thoughtful for a while.

'But something still doesn't feel right,' he said. 'I can't put my finger on it at the moment.'

He took a sip of his drink and tried to relax. A few minutes later their lunch arrived and they started to eat. Mark was still thinking, and Stephen gave him room to do that.

Suddenly he sat bolt upright, with his eyes going wide and dropping his fork to the plate.

'What is it?' Stephen said with urgency.

'Shh,' Mark replied under his breath, holding his finger up for silence. Immediately on high alert, he felt outwards, focusing his attention. Then he sensed it. Something very dark and evil was close by.

He turned around and scanned the vicinity, looking closely. After a few moments a dark humanoid shape moved slowly across the floor some fifteen metres away. As he focused on the shadowy figure it slowly began to gain definition and clarity, finally materialising into what looked like a frail old woman. Dressed in black, bent over and haggard, her features were hidden within the depths of her cowl. She walked slowly, hunched over her equally decrepit trolley, pushing it along in front of her.

Staring intently, at first glance you could easily mistake her for a harmless old woman in spirit just pushing her shopping trolley around in a shopping mall. But something was very wrong with the image, and Mark watched her closely as she slowly walked by in front of the food counter.

Keeping his eyes locked on to the image, knowing something wasn't right, his eyes followed her path. Just as she turned the corner he pierced the illusion. His eyes opened wide, and with the impact of a sledgehammer realisation suddenly dawned.

'My God,' he breathed. It was the Crone. An old lady of myth and legend, powerful and steeped in evil, Mark had not even been sure she existed. Until now.

He turned to Stephen and spoke.

'Stephen, watch me, please. Protect me from the people around us. I have to trance and deal with something. Don't disturb me, no matter what.'

'OK,' Stephen replied, concern showing on his features. But he knew better than to question Mark at this time. Answers would come later.

Mark immediately closed his eyes, knowing speed was of the essence, or else he might lose her.

Leaving his physical body he followed swiftly around the corner where she had gone and saw her up ahead, just about to disappear. Speed was paramount, and Mark flew after her at breakneck speed. He knew full well that this was maybe the only chance he'd ever have to deal with this rarely seen being before she vanished again completely.

Operating behind the scenes, the Crone spread and controlled evil wherever she went. No one ever really got to see her because she appeared only briefly within the shadows, causing mayhem and destruction in her wake, then vanished before anyone saw or knew she had been there. Hence her reputation had fallen into myth and legend.

Reaching out with one hand, he made a desperate grab for her arm. On making contact with her bony spirit flesh, Mark felt her power. The dark energy emanating from her froze his hands. A tatty moth-eaten veil fell to one side, revealing her face as she turned, and black inky eyes locked on to his. Old and haggard, with thin, aged lips and a toothless grin, her skin hung from her in flaps. White wispy hair clung to the bones of her skull, making her as ugly as she was evil.

Mark recoiled as her hideous features stared straight at him.

A struggle of titanic proportions proceeded, with massive exchanges of violent energy. Summoning all the power he could muster, Mark used every trick he knew.

The Crone slammed him with a bolt of dark energy, attacking yet simultaneously trying to dislodge Mark's grip and make her getaway. It was primal in its nature, with no finesse, but Mark hung on. His own light energy blasted back as he tried to maintain his grip and deflect her attacks at the same time. Sparks of energy flew about them sizzling in the air.

Dark clouds appeared, attempting to encase Mark, which disappeared as his own shields intensified and dispersed the darkness. Light and dark energy overlapped each other, striking shields and body parts with equal intensity, jolting on impact or sliding past with a hiss.

The struggle went on for minutes as light and dark energy was exchanged with devastating power. No one came near them. Unaware of the silent titanic struggle nearby, the people around, naturally, but with no awareness of why, avoided the area. The energy around crackled and spat, with ripples and waves radiating out. Mark could feel his physical body swaying on his chair and leaning precariously to one side.

In the recesses of his mind he heard Stephen calling his name, clearly alarmed at Mark's physical state as he jolted and swayed as though being physically hit.

Stephen's hand gripped his arm. Realising he may be roused from his battle and put in mortal danger, Mark roused himself just enough to whisper urgently so only Stephen could hear,

'Leave me.'

Having done all he could, he resumed full focus on his battle with the Crone.

Stephen's hand dropped away, a concerned expression on his face as he watched the toll on Mark's physical body.

Mark was reaching the point of exhaustion. But, so he realised, was the Crone. And neither had the upper hand, so evenly matched were they.

In desperation the Crone let go of her grip and made a desperate attempt at flight. Hitting him with a dark shield and stunning him, she flew in the opposite direction. Recovering swiftly, he shrugged past the barrier and leapt on her, knocking her to the ground.

Light cords wrapped around her head and neck as she struck the floor face down with one hand buried in her central core energy. She struggled to rise, and Mark instantly summoned a light barrier, slamming it into her and pinning her once more to the ground. Urgently he called out for help in his spirit voice and instantly powerful light beings, a form of police if you like, appeared at his side and took hold of her.

With nowhere for her to go, Mark released his grip and stepped back. The Crone, surrounded by a ring of light beings, was hauled up, securely bound and led away, disappearing moments later.

Still in spirit form Mark stood up, gathering his strength, and a kindly spirit guardian appeared. High in rank, and responsible for overseeing a great many things, he smiled at Mark.

'You did well. Thank you.'

'This was a test, wasn't it?' Mark replied.

'Yes. We didn't know the exact outcome. But we have been after her for a very long time, and you were put in her path.'

'Why are you still testing me like this?'

'Is it not the right time and place for all to be tested? How else are you meant to learn and grow? You are a warrior of light, and your training continues. This is the way it should be. You needed a new experience. One higher than you have dealt with before.'

Thoughtfully Mark looked at him. He was not sure how to feel at that moment, but was trying to find a way of feeling indignant.

The spirit guardian smiled.

'But we owe you our thanks. You did well. Thank you. Go back to your body and rest. Your journey is not yet finished.'

With that it vanished and Mark found himself back in his physical body, slumped and leaning over to one side.

On opening his eyes he saw Stephen leaning towards him with his arm outstretched to prevent him from falling over.

'Are you OK?' he asked, concern written clearly on his face.

'Yes, just exhausted. That was the hardest thing I've ever had to do,' he said with feeling.

Stephen's eyes opened wide as Mark recounted the sequence of events, leaving almost nothing out.

Stephen sat back and spoke.

'So it seems this *is* part of a bigger picture, then?'

'Yes, it is. We cannot discount this as being part of darkness spreading. And it appears, my ongoing training,' he added wistfully.

'So what will you do now?'

'Go home and rest. Then travel back to England. Let things settle down here. Maybe come back and check in a couple of days to make sure it's all OK before I leave. But it should be. I'm pretty sure it's done now.'

After taking a few moments to settle down, they stood up and made their way to the car and the appealing sanctuary of Stephen's home.

The next day they returned to the mall and things felt much better. The energy had lifted and felt lighter and more positive. The food court was fortunately free of angry aboriginal spirits or any other negative spirit.

With this positive update on the mall Mark was able to book his flight home, and the following day they found themselves back at the airport.

'Thanks, Mark, for coming,' Stephen said.

'No problem. You're welcome. It was good to see you again, and we did some good work here.'

Hugging him briefly, Mark continued.

'We'll speak later, when I'm back in the UK. Keep an eye on things and let me know if anything else pops up. There's more going on than just here so I have to get back and see what's happening. Take care, Steve.'

'You too,' he replied.

Three hours later Mark was sitting on the plane, wondering what would be next. Putting his concerns to the side for the moment, he lay back and fell asleep in minutes for the long journey home.

Author's Note

When an area is troubled with bad spirits, the inhabitants there can be affected. As can the land. The land can become sick, nature may not be able to flourish, plants may die, vegetation may run wild, and animals may hide and live in fear. People may become ill and bad luck may seem to affect many, with tempers and relationships fraying. This can be a result of the energy of the land and surrounding area becoming sick.

We are all energy. No exceptions. We are connected to everything. When the land we live on is sick we become sick. And things go wrong. That is one of the reasons why it's important to keep your energy positive and healthy. That not only benefits you, but it also has a knock-on effect on everything and everyone around you.

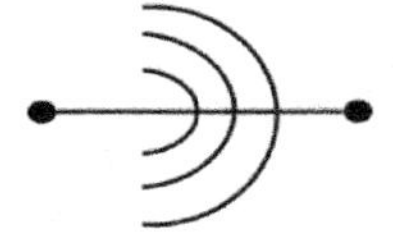

CHAPTER 10

THE COUNCIL OF ELDERS

The council of elders sat in a meeting with sombre expressions. Here was where much of the power was wielded. They sat, waiting expectantly.

Red Shaman stood in front of his peers, ready for the questions and decisions about his next tasks. While the members of his organisation sat alone, away from the usual machinations of the universal rank and file, he still had to answer for his actions.

The council of elders was nine in number for this meeting. The angel in the centre was older than the others. Though, to be honest, you would be hard pressed to tell, as, being immortal, they never appeared to age. But there was a greater depth and power that emanated from him.

'So, where are you now with his training?' this angel asked, looking directly at Red Shaman.

'All is going to plan, my lord,' he replied.

'Yes, we have seen your reports and viewed the transcript of events. We agree. But it is time to move him more towards the dark path. Work with our counterparts. He must learn control over the darkness. Once he has mastered that, we can look at the next stage. But first he must master his own darkness and control it.'

Red Shaman looked at his superior.

'Yes, my lord. That is not without risk,' he replied.

'We know. But this is as it should be. For him to become who we hope he will become, he must walk this path. If he can learn to control his own darkness and work with them without succumbing to the darkness he will be far more powerful in the end. This is but the first stage. If he passes this, we will look at taking him to the next level.

'Make the arrangements. We will be watching.'

Red Shaman looked slightly pensive as he answered.

'Yes, my lord.'

'That will be all.' The head elder gave a slight nod, indicating the meeting was over.

Red Shaman turned on his heel and walked out of the hall. This would be a big step for Mark. The trial would not be his ability to use dark forces and deal with them. He had already proved he could. Nor would it be him using more powerful dark forces to do his bidding in this escalating war. It would be how he reacted to that. Would he succumb to the darkness himself? Or walk the fine line of the middle ground and be able to work with both light and dark?

There is always a risk when working with darkness. It has an alluring nature, which appeals to the darker side of human emotion.

Red Shaman had chosen Mark well, and knew that he was a born warrior who was able to do whatever was necessary. But with that came a risk that appealed to his darker side.

Ego, anger and a burning desire to fight when provoked or needed: these were viable and necessary qualities that were required for going as far as he had gone and surviving. Tempered and balanced with more gentle and light qualities, they could lead to greatness. Creating a weapon of great power housed within a physical body that could fight for the light within the physical realms. But succumbing to the dark energies instead, would have the polar opposite effect and all would be lost. Red Shaman paused.

'Well,' he said. 'Let us begin this path and see where it leads. Be strong, Mark,' he pulsed out to the universe. 'Be strong.'

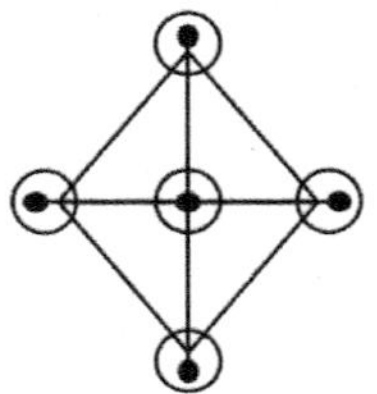

CHAPTER 11

HAUNTED HOUSE

A few weeks later Mark received a phone call from Dani, an old client of his. He knew her well and had assisted her on numerous occasions, helping both her and her family with various ailments over the years: some physical, some emotional and some past-life complications.

She had been an eager student, always asking questions and trying to learn more, and so Mark had become a willing teacher. He had also completed a full house-clearing a couple of times, and over the last few years regularly attended her house, cleaning the energies as her two children grew and developed from a very young age.

Dani lived in the depths of Berkshire. He always liked visiting this rural location and had a lot of time for her and her family. She greeted him as he picked up the phone.

'Hi, Mark, how are you?'

'Hey, Dani, I'm good, thanks. How are you?' Mark replied.

'Yes, good, thanks.'

'How's the house? The kids?'

'That's what I wanted to speak to you about. I think something is going on in the house. The kids don't feel well, and there are a few money issues. Richard is concerned about finances again. And Francesca is sensitive to things, as you know. She is complaining about being ill and things not feeling right in her room. I've talked to her about it.'

'Did you have a look?' Mark interrupted.

'Yes, but I'm not sure. Things aren't quite right with me, either. I seem to be struggling to connect to my guides and I don't trust what I'm feeling now.'

'How about Bob? How is he doing?'

'He is complaining that something is in his room as well.'

'I see,' Mark replied. 'It sounds like I need to come over and have a look, to be honest.'

'Yes, I agree. When can you come?'

'I can be over tomorrow morning if you like. I'm free tomorrow.'

'Thank you, Mark. You're so lovely. That would be great,' she said with feeling.

'No problem. About 10 a.m.?'

'Perfect. See you then.'

'Oh, one other thing. Would you send me some photos of the inside please? Several of each room and the communal areas. And also the outside gardens. It will give me a heads up of what is going on so I can prepare.'

'Yes of course,' Dani replied. 'I'll do that now.'

'Thanks, I'll see you tomorrow,' he said gratefully and hung up.

An hour later the photos arrived and Mark studied them carefully. Of particular interest was Bob's bedroom. The energy felt sick. But also something else was going on here. He could feel it. But no sooner had the feeling started to become clear, it drifted away like smoke in the wind. Closing the photos on his phone he thought about it for a moment. Knowing was tantalisingly close but he couldn't quite put his finger on it. Well he thought, I will find out tomorrow for sure.

Author's Note

Often before visiting a house with alleged energy/spirit problems the person assigned to deal with this problem will ask for photos of the property and surrounding land. Photos are very powerful, and much can be deduced from a photo concerning people, buildings and land. Even objects. The skilled medium and soul rescuer will use photos of the relevant point of interest prior to conducting a house cleansing or seeing if a person has attachments or negative energy about them. As always, the amount that can be found out and what information can be gleaned depends on the skill of the medium and his or her role at that time.

The next day Mark arrived at Dani's house and stood in the garden. It was a large six-bedroom property set in the heart of the Berkshire countryside and surrounded by gardens on all sides. Built in the 1930s, it was an established property with a lot of character. The gardens were impressive to look at and probably covered three quarters of an acre.

The large old wooden front door had an ornate brass knocker in the shape of a panther's head and Mark rapped it twice against the wooden panels. Moments later Dani answered. A tall, slim lady with a dark complexion and long black hair, she had an honest, open face and smiled welcomingly.

'Come in, Mark. Come in.'

She led him inside and Mark took his shoes off to protect the lush cream carpets. It was an unusual layout inside with no real structure to the rooms. They just seemed to be set at random places leading off a narrow hallway, with the main lobby area by the front door where he now stood. After taking him aside she brought him a cup of herbal tea, knowing his preference.

Mark was already starting to get a feel for the property inside and a minute later he was ready to look around.

'Why don't you show me around again and point out where you think the problems are?' he asked.

'Yes, of course,' she replied.

They walked around the house together and Mark picked up a general sense of the area. On stepping into Bob's room upstairs the energy changed significantly.

As soon as he tuned in Mark felt something sick in the corner.

'There's something not right there,' he said pointing to the offending wardrobe in the corner.

'That's where Bob says he thought something was in his cupboard. I've looked but can't really feel anything. I've just tried to reassure him.'

'I'll deal with that in a minute. Something is in there. Let's move around some more.'

Leaving some guards in place to seal the bedroom and prevent any escape, he continued to walk around the other rooms upstairs.

Upon entering the spare bedroom he could tell that a feeling of unhappiness and depression prevailed there.

'Is this room ever used?' he asked.

'No. I hang my pictures up here and sometimes we use the en suite, but no one sleeps in here. The children complain that they don't like it.'

'Yes, I can see why,' he replied, sticking his head round the door into the en suite. 'It doesn't feel great.'

When he moved into the other rooms, it was the same story. It varied in degree, but none of it was good.

When he walked downstairs it was more of a generic feeling, but the lobby area felt particularly bad.

'I think you're going to have to leave this with me now. You don't need to be in the house. Are you expecting anyone home?'

'No,' she replied, 'I don't have to pick up the kids from school till late this afternoon.'

'OK. It's up to you.'

'I'll pop out for a couple of hours. I have things I need to do.'

Turning round she made her way to the front door.

Once Dani had left, Mark tuned in properly. After sitting down he prepared himself. Then, deepening his breath and pulling in his power, he grounded and automatically called his spirit workers to him.

There was something nagging at the back of his mind, but he couldn't quite put his finger on it. With his awareness heightened, he walked around downstairs for a while, getting a closer feel of things, and then felt the need to go upstairs.

As he ascended the stairs the energy started to shift and became more negative. Calling down light and emanating it from within like a bright torch, he stood for a moment halfway up, changing the feel of the staircase till it lightened and lifted. Continuing up on to the landing, he walked into Bob's room.

Bob was a young, sensitive boy, and Mark had done his best to help and guide him through his younger years. He was able to 'see' and 'feel' things, and Mark knew he had the potential to do spiritual work later on in life if he chose.

As he looked straight at the wardrobe in the corner he knew instantly that this was the main source of the problem in the room. Something was in there. With his shields sliding into place, Mark opened the door and peered in among the clothes and various toys and boxes that children have. He could sense something hiding in the corner behind the clothes.

'OK, you can come out now. You're not meant to be here,' he said out loud.

It didn't move but stayed where it was. Mark could feel it as much as see it. Definitely non-human, it was a small demon, he surmised, which emanated a very negative energy.

Mark reached in, and grabbed it, took hold of its core energy and pulled it out into the open. Holding it fast, he took a better look. It was a black demon. Though small in physical size, it would nevertheless be the cause of all kinds of problems within the room. It would have been scaring the child and making the energy very sick, which the young boy would pick up on, potentially causing various adverse effects on him (fear, feeling unsettled, nervous, emotional, and even physically sick, to name but a few).

No wonder Bob didn't want to open the cupboard. Children are much more sensitive to spirits, energies and other non-physical beings than adults. This is because they are newer to their physical form, and retain a stronger connection to the energetic realms where their soul has just come from.

As they get older that connection weakens over time, as the pull of the physical world we reside in takes over. This is a progressive change, getting stronger over time, unless you are destined to be on a spiritual path, then the rules change slightly and you retain a stronger bond with the spirit and energetic realms. Or, like many, you may start to wake up later in life, and realise that there is more to what you see around you and start looking for answers.

Firming his grip, Mark quickly took stock. Indistinct in physical appearance but with a vaguely humanoid structure, it had a small body, with arms, legs and a non-human face.

No match for Mark, it struggled futilely to get away. After

passing it over to the waiting light guards, who took it away, Mark turned his attention back to the room. Channelling light specifically into the cupboard, he burnt away the negative energy till it was totally cleared. Then, focusing on the rest of the room, he repeated the procedure until that too was cleared.

Walking out into the hallway he crossed over to the double bedroom with the en suite that he had seen earlier. As he entered his attention was drawn to an armchair in the far corner of the room.

Something dark was sitting there, and he knew it shouldn't be. Raising his hands, light shot out and hit the entity, his light bonds wrapping around it. And Mark pushed. Nothing happened. His brows furrowed in slight surprise. Again he pushed, forcing more light down towards the entity, and again nothing happened. It didn't move.

Mark braced himself and pushed as hard as could, using all his considerable force. Yet still it didn't move. Concerned now, he stood back. His hands were still in place, with light shooting out from them.

Red eyes flicked open and bored into Mark's. Involuntarily Mark took a step back, shocked.

A fully fledged demon lord of the upper realms sat there, laughing.

'You can't move me, human,' it sneered in a deep voice.

Unable to do anything without help, Mark just stood there. No one else came to his aid and he was on his own.

'I will see you sooner than you think,' it said menacingly. Then vanished.

Mark dropped his hands and let out a sharp exhalation of breath. Something much larger than he had suspected was afoot. Had he not been certain before, he was now. What was going on here?

Gathering himself he walked around the rest of the house, disposing of minor-level demons and elementals till he felt the house was clear. Senses on high alert, he redirected his attention outside, projecting his non physical senses beyond the walls of the house. Something was out of sync. He could feel it. Decision made he resolutely made his way towards the front door.

Author's Note

It is worth noting that while we can develop our own inner power, and we should, ultimately there is a limit. Never forget that we are accessing source energy and using spirit's help and energy. Once we have reached our own personal limit, we rely on them to channel through us or lend us their power. Then it comes down to who you work with and who you can access.

Be under no illusion. Your role within this physical journey and how developed you are, both define who you work with. There is an entire hierarchy of infinite levels, from which certain beings will be chosen for you to work with.

Never allow ego to put you in a position of taking on something that you shouldn't. It is potentially dangerous for both you and anyone else around you. You could make the situation far worse.

Walk away. There is always someone who is suited for that job. The right person for the right task. The right tool for the right job. As it is in the physical world.

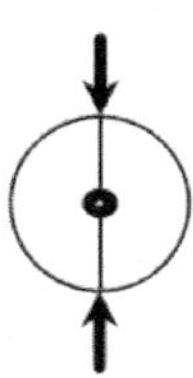

Chapter 12

The Portal

As Mark walked out Dani appeared in the drive.

Briefly he brought her up to speed, telling her everything but deciding to omit the incident in the spare bedroom upstairs. He'd deal with that later when he knew more. Right now he didn't have all the answers and didn't want to scare her.

'I have to look out here now, but you can go inside if you wish,' he finished.

Leaving Dani to go indoors, Mark stood outside in the front garden, looking at the front of her large house. As he tuned in to the land, he began sending his roots deep into the earth. As he did so he sensed something very wrong.

Pausing he looked intently at the house. Then the scene shifted. It was as though a veil was being lifted from across his eyes, like a heavy mist slowly clearing.

The calm scene in front of him turned to one of horror. A huge black portal the size of a crater appeared under the house, encompassing its entire base and beyond. His eyes couldn't believe what he was seeing as darkness seethed and boiled from within, and molten lava bubbled just below the surface, spewing fire intermingled with pure darkness.

Mark watched as the demon lord from earlier rose from the pit. Standing fully two thirds the height of the house its breadth of shoulders was huge, with thickly muscled limbs and a broad heavily muscled chest. Deep red eyes burnt out of its animal-like features and curved horns sat on top of its skull.

Mark was stunned. Never had he seen anything like this before. For a few moments he stood staring, stock-still. But then instinct took over. Gathering his power and grounding himself fully he summoned something from the depths of hell itself.

Dark and massive, a second demon lord slowly rose out of the ground and towered beside him. Authorised by the higher powers, it had the lawful authority to respond, and was answering Mark's call to return the usurper to the underworld from whence it came.

Equal in size to the first, it stared balefully at its opposite in the portal. Even blacker than the contender, its eyes gleamed a deep red and locked onto its opponent. Mark knew that the demon lord next to him had come at his bidding by universal law to deal with the contender. Enormous power emanated from it in waves and swamped Mark in dark energy. Almost immediately he became intoxicated with its power, as it sent shivers through his body.

They stood thus for several moments, their energies linked, and Mark revelled in the euphoria of battle lust and dark energy residing within this powerful demon lord at his side.

Then, as one, they attacked.

Feeling his light guards with him, their combined power merged with his, Mark raised his hand, and a light of immense power shot out and struck the demon lord full in the chest. It snarled on impact, and its head swivelled to take in this new threat.

Momentarily distracted, its attention diverted to Mark. Seizing the moment his demon lord roared its challenge and, with unbelievable speed far belying its size, charged the contender. Its huge form crashed into the usurper with earth-shattering force, knocking it to the ground, causing energetic ripples from the impact to reverberate across the vicinity. Mark's demon lord pounded the contender's head and body with massive fists, knocking aside the flailing arms that were desperately trying to dislodge its attacker and deflect the blows.

But the battle was far from over and the contender fought back. Twisting and surging upright, it regained its feet and both of them locked into a battle of pure strength and will. Mighty blows of immense power were exchanged as they both grappled and strained for supremacy. The contender pushed forward with a snarl and Mark's demon reacted with its own answering snarl, digging its heels in to hold the opponent at bay. Mark knew he would have been totally destroyed had he been on his own.

The battle swayed to and fro as mighty blows were exchanged. Dark energy and red-hot fire from open maws lashed at each other for minutes on end, with no side showing signs of clear victory.

Shock waves of dark energy, flattening everything in the vicinity, reverberated across the grounds from the titanic energy exchange between these two immense beings. Adding to his strength, Mark poured more power into his light beams. The demon lords were evenly matched and Mark was caught up in the euphoria of it all, so linked was he with the energies involved and with his own demon lord.

Through his haze and peripheral senses, Mark became aware that they were being observed by other powers, who were watching the monumental battle as an audience might watch two prize fighters on the physical plane.

He called out for more help with his spirit voice, and warrior angels appeared above him, immediately adding their power to his own. Reinforced with the angelic light coursing through him, Mark gathered himself, digging deep into his very soul and summoned every ounce of power he could muster. Both dark and light combined as he had never combined them before. His body glowed a brilliant white light, ready to explode, and just before he could take no more, he unleashed it all at the contender. Every bit. Searing white light screamed across the grounds and struck the contender full in the chest. The demon lord shuddered on impact as its power was weakened and muted.

Linked as they were, his demon lord roared simultaneously, and with a great surge struck the contender with a resounding crash, driving it back onto its knees. A feeling of desperation dawned, and wildly it fought back. Roaring, it spewed flames from its open maw, only to be countered by Mark's demon lord's own flames shooting back.

Slowly, inexorably, with Mark and his demon lord's combined powers, the contender was pushed further and further back towards the opening of the portal, until finally, teetering on the edge, it toppled over and sank down into the dark abyss below.

Mark's demon lord turned, locking eyes with him momentarily, and triumph blazed from within them. Then, without a word, it dropped down, following the contender into the darkness.

Mark stood for a moment in shock. Still linked to the demon lord's power, he fell to his knees as it dissipated and exhaustion took over. Shaking, kneeling on the ground, he bent over, trying to gather his strength. The observers had gone but he sensed that the light beings and the warrior angels who had helped were still there. Long minutes passed as he slowly recovered.

Hauling himself upright he knew he had one final task to complete. With the combined might of those with him, light burst from his hands as he closed the portal, covering it with a shield of white light. He expanded his light beams and directed them across the rest of the grounds, cleansing the entire area and removing the last vestiges of dark energy till it showed nothing but light where the portal had once been. Mark walked around the garden, mopping up any remnants, till no trace remained to indicate what had transpired.

His head sagged. Never had he been so exhausted. He walked into the house and sat down, slumping into a chair. Dani looked concerned as she brought him a glass of water.

After a few moments Mark gave a summary of what had happened. He omitted the more complicated details but supplied a synopsis, revealing there had been a portal beneath the property the size of the entire house, and that it had taken everything he had with all his helpers to close it.

'Wow,' Dani said. 'That must have been exhausting.'

'It was. I've never had to do anything like it before,' he said with feeling. 'But it's done now, and the house will improve. It will feel better. Give it some time and do the work I've taught you. Clear some old things away. Declutter. Meditate in the rooms to bring down some light.'

'And sage would help also.' He paused. 'Though that will smell the house out,' he said with a smile. 'Best do that when it's empty and you can open all the windows for a while afterwards. It won't stop this kind of thing or anything really serious. But it does help to keep the energy positive and good within the house.'

'OK, I'll do all that,' she replied.

After standing up he walked wearily to the front door and said his goodbyes to a grateful Dani. Leaving the house he climbed into his car and drove home.

As soon as he got home he threw his keys on the kitchen work surface and went upstairs. Stripping off his clothes, he left them where they fell and stepped into the hot shower, allowing the water to cleanse him for several minutes. Then, exhausted, he crashed on to the bed and slept through the afternoon and night.

Author's Note

There is always a risk when working with dark forces. Those who use dark forces for ill gain always have to trade off something for that help. Commonly something of themselves…their humanity, very often. Then there is a karmic debt to be paid.

At our core, we are light beings. Even the most 'evil' of us are light beings deep at our core. To play with darkness for ill gain is dangerous indeed, and there will always be consequences. Some, like Mark, are authorised by a higher power to use lawful dark forces in the universal battle against darkness. But the position is precarious.

Balancing light and dark is like walking a tightrope. Only the very strong can do this, and it is not without risk. Trying to hold on to your light and be that light being while constantly having to use dark forces at the same time, is a delicate and constant balance that will strain you mentally, emotionally, physically and spiritually.

The allure of darkness is strong, and many who tap into it to whatever degree succumb to its pull. It takes a great deal of willpower, self-belief, constant evolvement and work on who you wish to be. You need to constantly monitor and resist the pull.

Only a select few succeed. Only a select few are chosen.

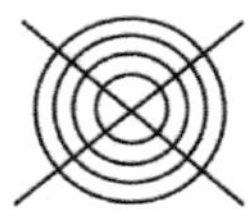

Chapter 13

Trials

Red Shaman stood with Abatheer and Malek, his underlings and colleagues. As they turned away from the viewing portal in front of them they took stock of what they had just witnessed.

'Well, that went well,' he said out loud.

Abatheer and Malek stood motionless.

'I think it's time for the next stage. Let's send him some more trials, and continue the use of the dark side. Let's get him totally embedded with the dark forces, to the point where he understands them all fully.'

Red Shaman looked over to his colleagues and with a wave of his hand, he spoke again.

'Go. Organise it.'

Abatheer and Malek looked at each other. Without another word they whispered in a language that had been dead for a thousand years. Their forms blurred and they vanished in a dark cloud, streaking towards some unknown place to prepare the scene.

Chapter 14

A Message

Things had been relatively quiet for the last few weeks. Mark was sitting down in his house, deep in meditation, when spirit came through and spoke to him.

'Go to a yoga retreat,' they said, in their typically direct manner.

'Really?' he replied 'Why?'

'There is work for you to do there.'

'Where?'

'Turkey. We want you to go to Turkey.'

'OK. I'll look into it,' he replied. 'Is there any more you can tell me?'

There was no reply, and, sensing that was all he was going to get, Mark finished his meditation and contemplated. The information he received had been specific. More specific than usual. They had told him where he needed to go and why. Generically speaking.

He smiled to himself.

'That was quite a lot, for them.'

Mark knew well that spirit often did not give you all the answers. If they felt you needed to know they would tell you. But the fact was that you usually got enough to work with and no more. You got what you needed to know rather than what you wanted to know. That was the way it worked.

Something was afoot, though, and it occupied his thoughts for the rest of the day.

Author's Note

Speaking to spirit is often much easier when in meditation, and this is the starting point for most people when they communicate with the spirit realms. With practice you can speak to them at any time during a meditation.

During a meditation, messages are generally conveyed in a different way from words. Often this is in a non-verbal manner and the message just appears in your mind, so to speak, without any words. Feelings and knowing are commonplace. With even more practice, of course, and a modicum of natural ability, you can learn to talk to spiritual beings outside meditation whenever you want to or need to.

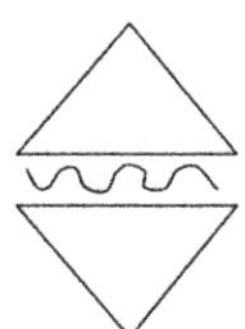

Chapter 15

Turkey

A few weeks later Mark was having a drink after a yoga class with the teacher. They had been chatting for some time and Mark liked her. Jane was a tall, slim woman in her mid forties, confident and still open to learning and growing. They had proved to be on a similar wavelength on a few things and she was keen to learn more about his spiritual world. The ramifications did not escape his notice when she brought up a certain topic and location.

'Mark, I am going to run a yoga retreat again in June this year. Would you be interested in coming?'

Mark thought for a moment and quickly came to a decision.

'Sure. Where will you run it?'

'Turkey,' she replied.

Mark paused and allowed the information to sink in. This was not happening by chance. But then, nothing ever really does.

'Sounds good. How much is it?' he answered.

'Well, that depends. I was thinking that maybe you'd like to teach a couple of sessions of meditation.'

'OK. Sounds like a good idea. I'm up for that,' he replied.

'If you came over and taught a couple of evenings of meditation, you could come for free and just pay for your flights and accommodation.'

Pausing briefly again, Mark smiled.

'That sounds like a great idea. I'm up for that. It could be a joint venture. It's your yoga retreat, of course, but if I can add something of benefit to your clients then everyone gets something from it. Yes, I'd love to.'

With the plan set in motion the finer details were sorted out over the next few weeks ...and Mark had not forgotten what spirit had told him.

Time flew by, and Mark soon found himself on a plane landing in Turkey. Having collected his luggage and exited customs, the prearranged hotel transport whisked him away to a beautiful retreat location in Dalyan, where he arrived an hour later.

He soon settled himself in and enjoyed the general ambience of the location and facilities. The staff were lovely and it wasn't long before Mark became a focal point for everyone when they found out his role at the retreat and field of expertise. A few days went by with yoga every morning and evening, and lounging by the pool in between. Sometimes they would all visit the nearby town or go on a tour somewhere locally.

It was on one such day that Mark got up and enjoyed breakfast before walking to the local river. There he joined an organised boat tour which would take them to a village that was famous for its thermal mud baths and natural springs.

He was excited about the trip and enjoyed the boat ride immensely. The rivers and lakes they sailed along were dotted with beautiful tall rushes, and you could hear the teeming wildlife within the reeds and flowers. Stunning cliff backdrops edged the scene as they rolled by.

An hour or so later they approached the village, and Mark was confronted with several beautiful hot spring areas. Visible were two natural mud baths encircled by ancient walls that kept the mud area carefully contained. A very old wooden pier led off into the sea, where he could see people jumping into the warm water.

A warning signal sounded in his mind, and he looked carefully around. Although he couldn't see anything obvious he acknowledged that something didn't feel right. Unable to pin it down, he shrugged it off, and continued to enjoy the hot springs and mud baths with the group. Caught up in the excitement of the afternoon, he almost forgot that nagging feeling in the back of his mind that triggered awareness and warned him that something wasn't right.

An hour later that nagging feeling, like a spider sense, returned in force as he walked towards a domed brick structure covering another natural hot spring. The structure looked well weathered and was clearly hundreds of years old, if not more. Visible evidence could be seen that it had been patched up and repaired over the decades to keep it operating and functional.

After walking under a low arched roof he entered the building. Other archways were scattered about the structure, and the surrounding bath floor areas were raised to different levels around the circular pool.

The pool itself was approximately twenty metres in diameter, and steam rose off its hot surface. The brickwork inside was clearly ancient, pitted and worn over time. Mark's senses were already heightened. The whole structure had an unearthly feel to it, and was very unfriendly.

Already in his swimming shorts, Mark walked over to the edge of the pool and slowly stepped in. The water felt soothing, and it was hard not to relax as his shoulders dipped under the steaming water. Three or four other people were in the pool, crouching down or lazily swimming from one side to the next.

He leant his back against the side and looked up at the domed walls and roof. Small alcoves were slotted at intervals into the ancient walls. Rough, pitted and old, they gave an off-putting feel to someone who was aware, and he idly wondered what they were there for. What purpose had these alcoves served? It seemed weird, and they were unlikely to be there just for aesthetic reasons.

He didn't have long to wonder. Looking around, he felt the vibration slowly shift as he gave it more attention and focus and honed into the energies within. The domed walls above held an almost hypnotic effect as he stared intently, unconsciously searching and feeling.

A dark shadow appeared above and gradually took form, coalescing into a figure seconds later. Other dark shadows appeared and also took form, appearing as if out of the very walls themselves. Mark found himself staring at numerous dark energy forms that almost melded with the walls themselves, watching and waiting like predators before they pounce.

The energy shifted and darkened, becoming more menacing.

Mark glanced around. People were still in the pool and on the poolside, totally oblivious of the shadows that were there or of the very real danger that they posed to their health and well-being.

'What am I going to do with these people all around?' he said to himself. 'I can't risk collateral damage with them here, or their seeing me doing things and wondering what the hell I am doing.'

Bringing up his protections he watched the shadowy beings slowly become more solid as they flicked across the walls from one alcove to another, only pausing to stare intently at him. They were some form of demon that he hadn't seen before, and were totally dark and malicious. He was in no doubt that an attack was imminent, and he was the prey.

After a semi-conscious call a fully fledged demon lord appeared alongside him. Mark instantly recognised it as the one he had worked with on numerous occasions before. Authorised by universal law for the greater good, he knew its energy as well as he did his own spirit guides.

Menacingly it glowered at the shapes flitting about across the walls. Powerful, and supreme in the belief of its own power, he could feel the desire to impose its will and take down these impudent demons in front of him.

Spirit responded to his concerns, and the people in the pool just drifted away until it was completely empty.

Looking up, Mark gathered his power. Intimately linked with the demon lord at his side in a way that is hard to describe, he felt its power and the total belief of its supremacy and strength. Its arrogance. The need to dominate and deal out mayhem and death to those that opposed him.

Allowing these feelings to wash through him, Mark shot beams of pure white light out of his hands and slammed into a dark figure on his left, pinning it against the wall and holding it fast.

Rushing forward at incredible speed, the demon lord tore into the dark ones in front of him. Taloned hands lashed out and tore into them, throwing them aside like rag dolls. Light shot out from Mark's hands at any targets caught in his sights and pinned them against the walls while the demon lord created mayhem among the others.

A black portal leading to the underworld opened up off to the side. The demon lord grasped them one after the other and dragged them down into it in ones and twos.

With his arms extended, and the demons bound by his beams of white light, Mark followed suit and started dragging them into the portal too.

Suddenly a demon escaped its bonds and leapt at Mark. Immediately sensing his danger, the demon lord reacted with incredible speed and Mark embraced its essence as they merged into one. Power and fury rose through him. How dare it?

Mark and the demon lord hybrid stepped forward to meet the attacking demon as one. Mark's hand shot out and grabbed the demon by the throat, stopping it dead in its tracks. It struggled futilely, but was no match for their joint power, and hung impotently in Mark's grip. With an almost negligent gesture Mark tossed the demon into the beckoning black hole next to him. Glancing briefly, he sensed outstretched hands waiting just below the portal surface ready to pull the hapless demons down into it.

With the imminent danger over, the demon lord separated from him and between them they disposed of the remaining demons. Mark was shooting light beams and hauling them into the waiting portal. The demon lord was laying waste to everything around him and hurling others into the beckoning darkness. To the last the demons fought, but finally they were all were dragged back down into the underworld.

With the last of them gone Mark looked about. He allowed his energies to settle down and become more … him. He looked over and watched the demon lord, silently acknowledging it. Without a word it stepped over the waiting abyss and disappeared from sight, the portal slamming shut as it disappeared from view.

Taking a moment to scan the area, Mark felt his energies shift. With the demon lord's disappearance and the immediate threat over, he felt the dark, intoxicating influence slowly filter out of his system. Directly he asked for light beings to come, who appeared almost simultaneously on his request. As he allowed his thoughts to track back during the battle, he realised that in fact they had always been there, in the background, hovering above the domed structure, silent but observing.

'So,' he pondered to himself. 'Was this another test? Were they just watching, ready to act only if needed? Or just observing me and the situation? Or both?'

The realisation dawned upon him that again this was part of a bigger picture and he was directly involved. They were observing him and testing him.

'So be it,' he thought.

Now he knew why he had been sent there. It didn't matter whether they would have intervened or not. It was all about the test, and, he guessed, the training.

With that settled in his mind, Mark brought his attention back to the room and checked that the energies were changing to a more positive and a lighter vibration. He could see the light beings doing their work. The place was secure now. It would take time, but already he could feel the shift.

Knowing he could leave, as his work there was done, he made his way out of the building into the fresh air.

When he extended his senses he could feel that the energy of the whole area had changed slightly and was more positive. As he walked back towards the waiting boat he glanced at the domed building and could see the energy colours lift around it. They were less imposing and more friendly in feel. His job here was done.

Author's Note

Jinn are generically another name for a dark, malicious spirit. Mainly used within the Islamic cultures.

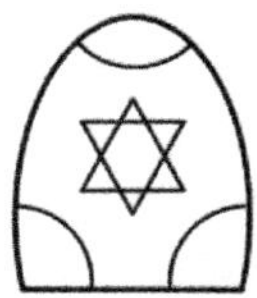

Chapter 16

Symbols

Mark woke up back at the retreat and decided to have a proper walk around the grounds the following morning. Numerous two-storey buildings and chalets surrounded a tranquil pool area in no apparent order. On one side of the grounds was an open-air yoga studio, and some huts that could be used for therapies or other suitable purposes. A dining area was situated to the north side with a snack bar opposite, close to the pool, with tables, chairs and a lounging area inside. Overall it was a small and cosy retreat centre and seemed very pleasant.

It was there that Mark found himself chatting to Azra, one of the managers of the centre. In her early forties, slim, with dark hair and an endearing smile, they had chatted several times before and he had found that she had a strong interest in all things spiritual, particularly within the spirit realms themselves. The conversation took on a surprising turn when she told him that they had the area cleared of bad energy by a local Turkish shaman.

'OK,' he replied. 'That sounds good. When was that done and what did he do? Was there a problem?'

'Well,' she replied, 'the business was struggling a little

financially. The owner decided to have the energy cleansed in case there was a problem with that.'

'What did he do?'

'The shaman came over and did some work. He walked around the grounds saying there was a bad Jinn that he had removed, and he'd cleared the energy. But he also said that he had left some symbols on the ground in different places to keep the bad Jinn away. To be honest, I didn't like him very much and didn't trust him. There was something wrong about him, and he was very arrogant. I don't trust what he did.'

'That does sound weird. Do you know where he put the symbols?' Mark replied.

'Yes, I'll show you. One of them is under a chair in the lounge area by the snack bar inside. I don't like the way it feels in there.'

They walked over to the lounge and stepped inside. Azra pointed out the armchair and Mark walked over to it.

'I don't even like coming to the snack bar now,' she said earnestly. 'It feels bad to me and I don't like it so much in here either,' she continued, with distaste written across her features.

As soon as he honed his senses Mark noticed the shift in energy. Approaching the corner with the armchair in, he gradually started feeling sick. The closer he got the stronger the intensity was.

Taking hold of the chair he pulled it away. The chair had been hiding a black symbol written on the tiled floor, which was protected by some form of hard plastic cover. Now exposed, the energy became even worse and the sick feeling inside him intensified. His features screwed up as though there was a bad smell. After pulling down his protection he tentatively reached out and touched the symbol with his hand. The negative dark energy poured off it in waves, making him recoil swiftly.

Steeling himself, he touched it again and found the plastic cover stuck fast.

Turning back to Azra, he said,

'It's very sick. This is not good in any way.'

'I tried to remove it once but couldn't get it off, and it made me feel so bad I stopped and never went back. I've made sure the chair is always on top of it,' she replied with a shudder.

'Wise decision,' he replied. 'It's very sick and you shouldn't touch it. And it was a wise move, keeping the chair over it. That helps mute the energy. You say the shaman put it there to keep bad energy and Jinn away?'

'Yes.'

'That's not what it's doing at all. Give me a moment. I'll try to find out what's going on here.'

Standing still, Mark closed his eyes and focused, mentally asking for answers and allowing them to flow to him.

A minute later he opened his eyes and looked at Azra.

'This has been placed here to generate negative energy. It is also somehow giving the shaman power over this place. He can feel things through these symbols he's placed around. Do you have a photo of him somewhere?'

'Yes, he has a website.'

She got her phone out and searched for the website, and moments later showed Mark a portrait photo of the man. He studied the photo intensely. Dark and swarthy, with cold black eyes and short black hair, the feeling coming from him was negative and dark. Born of arrogance and naturally manipulative, he had placed the symbols about the grounds, linking himself to them somehow. He was using them to gain power and control of the energies within the retreat, and to observe what was going on there.

Mark told her what he thought.

'Also,' he continued, 'he wants to keep the place to himself. To maintain a measure of control for his own ends. He wants to be the only one you call to come here and sort out any problems, thereby maintaining his control and keeping money flowing to him.'

Azra looked at him wide-eyed.

'He did say he wanted to come back to make sure everything was OK. I managed to persuade the owner not to call him again.'

'You did the right thing,' Mark replied. 'I'm going to fix these symbols.'

Gathering his power, Mark spoke to his guides. He had dealt with symbols before. Dark magic, voodoo and many other forms had all crossed his path before. Always he let spirit come in fully to guide and deal with it.

'How do we do this?' he asked the silent question.

As he thought of previous times he had dealt with similar things an idea came to his mind.

'We will guide you,' replied the collective group who answered many of his questions.

Feeling his power rise, he placed his hands over the symbol and light blazed from them as he allowed spirit to work through him. Moving his hands over the affected area he began to erase the symbol, removing its energetic power. He stood thus for several minutes, until, after finally feeling its power leaching away, he dropped his hands and surveyed his handiwork.

The dark energy had been removed, to be replaced by a totally neutral feel.

Turning to Azra, he said,

'I have neutralised it. It has no power now and is in a neutral state. I would still remove it, though. You'll have to peel off that plastic cover and rub the symbol off. Are there any others?'

'Yes, there are a couple of others.'

'Show me where they are,' he commanded.

Azra walked with Mark as they walked around the retreat's grounds and he repeated the same procedure with three other symbols. All emanated the same negativity.

Standing back, he said,

'That's the last of them?'

'Yes, I think so.'

'OK. I'm just going to check the grounds,' he replied.

With that Mark walked off, carefully extending his senses and looking for any negative spots or problems within the grounds. Finding one area by a relatively unused therapy hut he cleared and neutralised the energy, transmuting it into positive. While mopping up he found two unwanted dark elementals that were sitting in some sick energy pools nearby. He removed them with relative ease and then cleansed the pools, making them positive and light. He continued his walk but found no more problems. The rest of the grounds appeared to be clear.

Satisfied, he returned to Azra and informed her about what he had done.

'Thank you,' she said, 'That's very kind of you. I'm so glad you sorted out those symbols. It felt horrible to me there, and I just didn't want to go anywhere near them. I avoided them completely.'

'No problem. You may find you receive contact from this shaman now. He may pick up on what's been done, or notice that something is wrong. He'll want to re-establish his control here and ask questions about what was done. He'll try to persuade you to use him again so he gets more money. Don't let him come back, or else you will have the same problem all over again. It's up to you whether you tell the manager or not.'

She momentarily hesitated.

'I'll just tell her you cleared some negative energies from the place. I won't tell her anything else. She's not as open as I am about these things.'

'That's a good idea. Well, I'm glad I was here to help,' he said with a smile.

Mark turned around and made his way back to his room and lay on the bed. Everywhere he went, it seemed, there was a job to do. This was no coincidence. He didn't believe in them anyway. He knew everything happened for a reason. No exceptions, even down to the most minor detail. Although many things that happened were just part of a bigger path, and not intrinsically significant on their own, still, nothing happens by accident. There is always a meaning, a reason, a lesson, or personal growth to be attained as a result.

With that thought in mind he fell into a satisfied sleep.

The rest of the week passed with little of consequence happening, and it wasn't long before Mark found himself saying his goodbyes and promising Azra he would stay in touch. He had enjoyed her interest in his work and all things spiritual, as well as answering her questions and deepening her understanding, so he fully intended to stay in touch if she so desired.

The flight home to the UK went without incident and Mark arrived home composed and relaxed.

But it didn't last long. It almost never did.

Author's Note

Just because you call yourself a shaman or healer, a doctor or counsellor, or consider yourself to be religious or not religious, or anything else for that matter, it doesn't mean you're a good person. They are just badges, labels, if you like, that you have put upon yourself.

What makes you a good person, any person, comes from within. Always trust how you feel. If that feeling doesn't feel right it probably isn't right.

Listen to that feeling.

Chapter 17

Training

For the next year Mark had more and more confrontations across the country. Dark forces had increased their attacks, and he was called upon time and again to thwart their plans. Some were minor, others were significantly more serious. During this constant period of conflict Mark developed a natural affinity in working with his own dark forces to combat them, and, as a result, he found himself increasingly fighting darkness with darkness. Frequently using extreme violence and aggression without hesitation if required, believing he was justified in doing so. The beings he used were subject to universal law and allowed to be used under that law. Just as light beings are.

Over time, with the constant battles, it became almost his default setting to use a dark being as his weapon, so to speak, tapping into his own darkness to do so. Always using a more powerful being than the ones he would confront.

That isn't to say that he didn't use light beings. Of course he did. But his default action would be to use a dark lord each time he was confronted with another powerful dark being. As a great master had once said to him,

'Who better to deal with a demon than another higher, more powerful demon?'

Due to Mark's natural warrior personality it was an easy path to follow. But underneath it all he felt that something wasn't quite right. After winning one particularly vicious confrontation, dark activities seemed to subside considerably for some months, and Mark found he had time for introspection. He had felt some changes going on within himself. And they didn't feel great.

Ill at ease sometimes, he felt unsettled, and noticed things didn't feel right within himself. He couldn't ground down the left side of his body properly, and noticed that the energies would bounce up and down like a yo-yo through his body and leg when he tried. This tended to be his light feminine side, he knew, and he felt his connection changing, both with spirit and within himself.

For weeks he tried to analyse what was going on but could not get to the bottom of it. Weeks turned into months. Perplexed by the situation, he turned to one of his original teachers, who had also become a friend, and gave her a call. Although she had not seen him for some time she still knew him well, and advised him to come to a retreat in southern England.

Two weeks later Mark prepared himself and drove down to the bed and breakfast where he would stay for the long weekend, ready to see where this would all lead.

The first afternoon Mark met up with his old teacher, Jane. She ran these retreats with her husband, also a powerful force within the same field as Mark, who had been his mentor.

Jane was a tall, imposing woman with a no-nonsense yet kind demeanour. She sat in front of him, waiting expectantly.

Mark explained what was going on.

'I have tried everything,' he said earnestly. 'I've used all my abilities and I cannot seem to fix this grounding problem. I've never had it before. The energies bounce up and down like a yo-yo, and despite all my training I can't seem to fix it.'

Encouraging him to go on, Jane nodded.

Mark hesitated. He knew that whilst Jane was a capable healer and had some understanding of the dark realms, this was not exactly her field of expertise, and he desperately wanted to be understood.

'I have also been using more dark beings when I am working, and I can feel their pull on me now. It doesn't feel quite right. I feel … off. Unbalanced somehow.'

Jane thought for a moment, then replied.

'It's as if the dark beings you work with have taken almost complete control. You are indeed out of balance. You need to bring in more light and regain your equilibrium. I want you to meditate on this and see what answers you get. Tomorrow you will sit in the woods and connect with nature.'

The following morning Mark sat cross-legged in the woods. With his eyes closed, and sending his energy down into the earth, he entered a trancelike state in which his soul connected to source energy. For some time he sat thus, clearing all thoughts and physical discomforts from his being and attained a peaceful zone of emptiness.

Visions and thoughts entered his being as his life played out in front of him. He was forced to confront his weaknesses and fears. His ego. His anger. His desire for battle.

Everything was shown in clear definition as scenes from his past ran through him. Past lives were displayed without mercy, showing clips of his nature and who he was.

A soul of extremes, he knew nothing else. In these previous

lives he was almost always a warrior of some description. Samurai, ninja, and assassins were prominent amongst them. But not only.

In one past life he was even a tyrannical warlord in Mongolia centuries before, and had been responsible for the death of thousands. In other lives, to counterbalance this, he had lived the life of a holy man or a monk. Some he had sat in the mountains living out his entire life in prayer and servitude as a monk of some description.

In this life his faults were shown in stark reality. He had been given a hard life in some respects, and in others, a good one. He remembered that as a young boy he had nightmares and would lie in bed seeing dark shadows hiding and watching, flitting around his room trying to attack him. Floating above, hiding behind curtains, darting in and out, they were like predators waiting for the right moment to strike. Young Mark had imagined placing shields around his bed to protect himself, and fearfully hiding behind these imaginary shields. Little did he know that even then he was actually placing real shields around himself.

He had been socially challenged and had always struggled to make friends and mingle with other children, and some attempts were even made to bully him. He didn't understand why, though he felt different to others and often isolated.

But there was always something about him that stopped the bullying going very far. He had a quality that put fear into others that neither he nor they understood.

The same had happened as a young adult. Not willing to toe the party line, he became a target to some people. He became harder and harder as a defence mechanism, and routinely used anger and fear to deal with challengers. His willingness to do harm to those who had wronged him became automatic when needed, and people recognised that within him.

Revenge. Justice. An eye for an eye. All these were words and expressions that he believed in.

The price of all this was digging into his inner self and embracing his survival instincts, his darkness. He pushed aside any feelings of gentleness and love and trained his physical body to be strong and powerful. By tapping into his dark side, using anger, personal power and ego, he learnt to survive and succeed. The offer of violence always hovering just below the surface. He became a force to be reckoned with and feared by his opponents.

Mark sat and watched the scenes roll by, feeling despair as his past streamed across his vision. Recognition of who he was brought shame, sadness and regret, and a single tear rolled down one cheek.

Then the scene shifted and realisation came to the fore. Only his iron control, integrity and belief in doing what was right had held that dark side in check, had made the difference between being a villain and being a force for good. Never had he deliberately wronged someone first. Never had he started a physical confrontation. Neither had he sought it. He had always been willing to help others in need or in trouble. The dark aspects of self, coupled with his iron sense of integrity and honour, had made him the perfect soldier to fight for light against the darkness.

Then spirit spoke.

'You have become a master of fighting darkness with darkness. You need to lay down your swords, your weapons. Get in touch with your light, and, over time, you will learn to use the power of the light. Then you will become far more powerful than you are now.'

Mark was profoundly touched and a deep understanding began to grow within as he absorbed these revelations, and spent the rest of the retreat in contemplation and ritual, analysing what this meant for him.

As he left the retreat the following day a sense of purpose came over him, and over the next twelve months he was put in many dangerous situations. Spirit stripped him of his weapons of darkness. He could see the dark ones, beings of great power he had been working with, just to the side. Held back behind a shield of light, they could no more come to him than he could them.

Regularly wondering how he was going to do his job without his tools, he continued working anyway.

Time and time again, Mark was given jobs, clients and experiences that had been set to challenge him. The underworld soon learnt of his perceived weakness and challenged him on a regular basis.

On one such occasion he was attacked by a powerful demon while looking at a new-build home.

As soon as he entered the property to look around he felt uneasy. That unease increased as he wandered around the house room by room. By the time he got to the top floor that feeling had increased to such a degree that he knew he had to get out. And quickly, knowing full well that something was there and an attack was imminent.

Deprived of his usual weapons, he walked swiftly down to the first floor. By the time he got there the situation was no longer in doubt, and a mild feeling of panic came over him. On reaching the last stairway the danger felt all too real, and way too close, and he started to run down the stairs, taking two or three at a time. Feeling a large demonic presence right behind him he went into full flight mode, and his fear was now very real. Frantically casting a glance behind him he fully expected to be caught and his headlong flight gathered pace.

Fortunately, unbeknown to him, he was being observed and protected. His new guardian angel suddenly appeared, glowing a brilliant white, and placed a shield of light on the landing behind him. The impenetrable barrier brought the demon's pursuit to an abrupt halt as Mark, almost running at break neck speed now, exited out of the front door with an explosive breath. He distinctly remembered turning round and the extreme feeling of relief he felt when he saw the guardian angel place the shield. The demon, howling in frustration at his escape, was still pounding on the invisible force field.

But that was the way of it. Time and time again he found himself challenged and having to deal with experiences without his usual weapons, having to find new ways of doing things. He was regularly confronted with dark beings who knew only too well that he was in a weakened state.

He also found he had to work on himself and needed to change things within. There was an adjustment of thinking. Of being. And it was a slow process.

But, for each challenge and confrontation, he found a way. While only working with light, he found the light within.

Always he could see or sense the lawful dark beings he had worked with in his peripheral vision, waiting to be called upon. Wanting him to call on them. Promising help with the allure of sanctuary and safety. But not once did he use them. Always the light stepped in just enough to protect and help him succeed. And he always did.

Over time he was given new abilities, new guides. Access to new light beings. Some in forms and ways he had never seen or heard of before. As his strength grew the attacks by dark forces gradually stopped. Always sensing the lawful dark side in his peripheral vision, they too stopped calling for him.

Many months later, when spirit decided he was ready, they allowed him to access the darkness. But always it was brief, as though they were testing him. And always he would send them back to where they came. Behind the light barrier.

The rules of using darkness gradually eased as his natural use of light came to dominance and his own shift came within. Towards the end of his training, while he was with a client who wanted to learn about the world of dark beings, he felt the urge to channel information. He had also observed a powerful demon appear by her side, one that should not have been there but had been bold enough to appear in front of him. He could feel its challenge.

Sitting down to focus, Mark opened himself up, and a being of unquantifiable power came through. Feeling dizzy and totally ungrounded, his head swam and his body swayed. Almost overwhelmed by its immensity, with a huge wrench he managed to gain some stability and focus. And with intense shock he realised what it was.

The lord of darkness. Chaos itself. In the same way that source, the divine, God, whatever you wish to call it, was the origin of light, this was the origin of darkness. Pure, unadulterated darkness. The ultimate power of the darkness of the universe itself. The counterpart of light.

Its power was immeasurable and he'd never felt anything like it before.

He could feel it was lacking the usual negative aspects of darkness. It was above all such petty emotions. Struggling to keep grounded and channel the information, Mark realised that he was only feeling a tiny fraction of its power. It was all his human form could take. Any more would completely overwhelm him and potentially drive him into a non-functioning wreck, or even madness.

Using his body as a vessel to communicate, Mark allowed it to speak through him. The Mark/Chaos hybrid looked momentarily across at the demon next to his client and briefly locked eyes. The demon simply vanished. Instantly. Another demon, previously unseen by Mark, stood off to one side. Braver than the other, or maybe more stupid, it didn't move.

Turning its attention to the other demon, the Lord of Chaos, pure darkness itself, looked at it for a moment. Then it said in a powerful voice,

'Really?'

The demon vanished, a sense of terror trailing behind it.

Slowly turning its attention back to Mark and his client, it spoke.

'If you wish to deal with dark beings you have to understand the nature of darkness. There is a danger to this. You must be careful. They will lie. Cheat. Test you and turn things to their own advantage. It is their nature. Although you can train a lion from a cub and have it under control, there will always be a chance that it will attack you. It is in its nature. Such is the way with dark beings. Some more than others. All are different. But you must be aware that it is a fine line to walk and can be very dangerous. Even when working with lawful dark beings, under universal law, there is a risk. An attraction to the dark side. It is a dangerous place to work. Be warned.'

With that, prime darkness, as that is what he later chose to call it, slowly left him. Mark was in shock and it took some minutes for him to recover and gather himself. He knew the message had been as much for him as for his client.

For weeks after that Mark pondered the meaning of this visit by prime darkness, the origin of darkness itself. He was trained now only to use light in almost all circumstances, and he knew that he had been shown something of major importance.

Then he understood. He had evolved and changed enough for a new level to be reached. His power had grown. New guardians and beings of light had been given, new powers and abilities learnt.

He now had access to both light and dark.

Chapter 18

The Balance of Light and Dark

Red Shaman stood in the clouds where none could see except those who were meant to. Pleased with Mark's training, he knew the members of the council of elders were watching, and Mark had to be ready.

'Time to move forward to the final stage,' he whispered, and said a prayer into the wind.

Things were set in motion that had always been preset and ready for this exact time, he knew. But still, nothing was ever really certain. An infinite number of variables still had to be considered. Events could always change. He had done what he could.

With a whispered thought of command, beings of ancient origin whispered their reply in a language known only to their master, and with a high-pitched wail streaked down towards Earth to set the scene.

CHAPTER 19

ANOTHER MESSAGE

One week later Mark rose from his night's slumber, threw on his dressing gown and went downstairs. His two cats greeted him, crying noisily for their breakfast, which he dutifully supplied, and was rewarded with a mixture of contented sounds coming from them as they ate. Smiling, he prepared his tea and walked into the lounge to sit and practise his usual morning meditation before making his own breakfast.

After finding his rhythm and grounding, within moments Mark sat in his peace, in that zone where you let go of the physical, shut out the outside world and connect with source, your inner self, and spirit. This is the reason for meditating. It is this place, this zone of inner peace and tranquillity, that we all desire to achieve within our meditation. It brings great harmony to the body, mind and spirit. This in turn has a very real effect on our physical health and well-being, emotionally and mentally. Mark strived to do this every morning so that he was set for the rest of the day.

Gently spirit let their presence be known. Unsaid greetings were exchanged, feelings and knowing instead of words. Then they spoke.

'Thailand. We wish you to travel to Thailand.'

'Why?' Mark pulsed back.

'There is a job for you there. A darkness has risen.'

Mark thought for a moment.

'Darkness. But why there? What's special about there?'

'It is connected with the dark lord. And it's an important experience for you. Something different. A lesson to be learnt.'

They left it there for a moment as Mark pondered over what he had been told. He knew it was important, or else they wouldn't have brought it to his attention and asked him to go there.

'We will arrange for things to fall in place so you can go. Do not worry. Just go.'

There was finality in their words and Mark understood.

'Thank you,' he replied, and they vanished.

Returning to his zone of peace Mark continued his meditation and after a substantial amount of time had elapsed he reluctantly brought himself out. Focusing on his breath and reaffirming his connection with the earth through the soles of his feet, grounding and orientating himself, he returned to the present and now so he could operate on a physical level.

Opening his eyes he took a few deep breaths. Feeling refreshed and at peace within, he thought about what he had learnt. There was no doubt he would go to Thailand now. He had been there several times before and looked forward to this opportunity to revisit the country. He had no idea where he had to go or what experience awaited him. But he knew, without doubt, that he would find out.

A week later Mark was on a flight to Bangkok. He had cleared his diary, hastily rearranging his clients. He still had no idea what would happen when he arrived but trusted the answers would come. Or else it would be much more of a holiday than he expected. Comforted with this thought, he settled down and closed his eyes and fell asleep within minutes.

The rest of the journey continued without mishap, and after landing he caught a taxi parked outside to drive him to his hotel. A short journey of some thirty minutes or so saw him pulling up outside a flamboyant hotel aptly named Dreams in the centre of Bangkok. Blue neon lights adorned the frontage and the name of the hotel was displayed prominently in bright glittering lights. As he stepped through the swinging glass door he could see the extravagant decor inside.

After checking in Mark took the lift up to the fifth floor and swiped his electronic key to enter the room. Blue neon lights were also in prolific use inside the room as a show of yet more glitz, but Mark felt comfortable inside.

Throwing his suitcase on the bed he jumped into the shower, got changed, and was soon stepping out into the hustle and bustle of Bangkok nightlife. The atmosphere was heavy and humid. Street vendors peddled a multitude of diverse goods and services, from clothing and fake jewellery to psychic readings and tarot. Taxi and excursion owners touted for business whilst numerous street food vendors offering their culinary delights were dotted along the roadside. Wafts of heavy, pungent odours drifted up from sewage openings set at regular intervals in the pavements. Many were partially covered with bits of old disused cloth or carpet in an attempt to keep the stench at bay.

A mass of jumbled electric cables were hung above the roads, looking like spaghetti with no apparent order to them. The pavements were heavy with pedestrian traffic, but no one bumped into each other and the energy was good. Thailand was Mark's favourite country as there was a distinct lack of aggression and anger over there and the land just felt peaceful. You could feel it as soon as you got off the plane.

Mark made his way to his favourite backstreet restaurant, one where all the locals and seasoned travellers ate. It was nothing to look at – in fact it looked grimy and grubby – but the food was amazing, and cheap. After ordering some rice and chicken Mark enjoyed the ambience. His food was quickly served and he ate with relish as he lazily watched the people go by, allowing himself to relax and his mind to detach. A feeling came to him, a knowing, if you like, that he needed to meditate.

After finishing his meal he left the restaurant and strolled down the main road till he found a small square with a Buddha statue surrounded by candles and open containers of drink. Straws were crammed into bottlenecks and can openings and several benches lined the outside of the square. Many such places existed around Bangkok. They were considered holy, and the local community used them for prayer, praying for loved ones, prosperity, health and happiness, and whatever else they desired. This evening though, the square was empty as he entered and Mark sat down.

After closing his eyes and settling swiftly into a meditative state he found himself undisturbed and answers forthcoming. Spirit spoke.

'You will travel to Kanchanaburi. There we have something for you to do.'

'How will I get there?'

'All will be arranged.'

A vision appeared in his mind of a hotel in a quiet town, and he knew that the arrangements would be made. Conversations were often short and always to the point with spirit. Well used to this, he was not fazed by their abrupt disappearance. Instead he liked it. It was concise and uncluttered. Perfect. Well, most of the time. It could be a little frustrating on the odd occasion when they were less than forthcoming or a little cryptic. But going with the flow and relaxing was the key. And in this he was well practised.

Author's Note

Grounding

This is a common term used by many. It means to connect your energy field with the Earth's energy field. Being grounded is the opposite of being all over the place like a headless chicken. It helps you be focused, connected, able to concentrate and think in a stable manner. It is typically done through the soles of your feet connecting to the earth.

Chapter 20

Kanchanaburi

Mark checked out of Dreams and the concierge phoned for a taxi to take him to Kanchanaburi.

The journey was relaxed, and two hours later Mark was in a small town very different from the bustling streets of Bangkok. Although orientated around tourism it was still much quieter. Everything was just on a smaller scale. Even the streets were narrower, and had fewer vehicles. Local shops and restaurants touting for business lined narrow footways.

Mark had not booked anywhere to stay or even looked at possible places so the taxi driver drove around, stopping at several hotels to check them out. Mark dismissed all of them till at last he found a quaint single-storey hotel set right on the River Kwai. After paying the taxi driver he booked himself a large double room and settled into the beautifully decorated accommodation. A huge bed graced the centre of a spacious main room which led off into an equally large en suite. French doors opened up onto a private wooden veranda and views of the communal gardens. Great attention to detail had been taken by the staff to make it warm and inviting, and Mark liked it.

After a hot shower to refresh himself he decided to take a stroll outside. A man-made miniature river, teeming with flowers and water life, flowed around the premises, and the energy was very much one of peace and harmony.

As he turned the corner on the main path he was presented with the historic River Kwai. A wooden pier extended into the waters and he walked onto it. The huge river was quiet, with just a few boats travelling along its length. Mark sat down cross-legged at the end and looked around. The sun was beaming down. To him the scene was beautiful. The sunlight bounced off the moving waters, causing cascades of shining light. The hotel grounds were just behind him, and meandering pathways lined with flower beds showing glorious bright colours could be seen. He felt at peace.

Closing his eyes, he absorbed the energy of the land and quickly sank into deep meditation.

Once there spirit connected with him. But this time it was no ordinary spirit. A vast presence brushed his mind. Allowing his senses to feel the presence, Mark felt pure light and love emanating from the being. But with this came a sense of overwhelming power so strong it was untouchable. Rather than aggression or arrogance used as its power, love, kindness and caring poured from within. And its power was that of love and light. This was the spirit of Thailand itself.

Bathing in its presence and humbled, Mark waited silently, watching and feeling. He could see the presence in his mind's eyes in the distance, like a great white energy source pulsing.

'You will go to a temple, and there you will learn your lesson and help us at the same time.'

An image was placed in his mind of an ancient natural rock cave temple on the river.

Sitting in awe of the spirit of Thailand, Mark silently acknowledged his task. He knew that everything would be provided for him to visit this temple tomorrow. The spirit sent his blessings and slowly withdrew, leaving Mark in a state of bliss as he absorbed what had just happened.

Never had he spoken to a single deity that was the essence of a whole country before. And its energy was such that it explained much about why he felt so comfortable in this country.

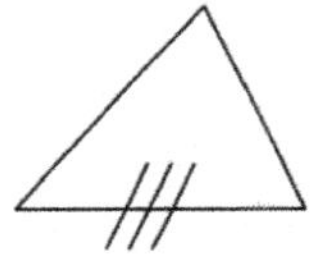

CHAPTER 21

THE TEMPLE

The next morning Mark had his breakfast by the small river that flowed around the hotel while enjoying the view, and then ambled towards the reception where he enquired if they knew of a natural rock cave temple. The staff said they did. It was a well-known Buddhist temple not too far away, and they arranged for a boat to take him there an hour later, which would leave from the pier at the edge of the hotel. After thanking them he made his way back to his room, and a short time later walked down to the pier.

A long narrowboat duly arrived at the appointed hour and Mark climbed on board as it rocked gently from side to side against the old wooden structure. A single man at the rear of the boat held a rudder, which guided a large, noisy engine with a long propshaft two or three metres in length, culminating in a propeller that powered the boat.

Once Mark had sat down the boat driver twisted the throttle and the engine roared into life. The front of the boat rose up as they moved forward along the Kwai. Soon they were moving along the quieter, more scenic waterways with fewer boats and more rural surroundings. Sitting on the flat wooden seat Mark watched the river banks slide by and the natural, relatively unharmed Thai scenery, as yet unspoilt by modern civilisation. The sun was shining as the boat glided gently across the swells of the river and Mark smiled, enjoying this moment of beauty and tranquillity.

Forty-five minutes later the boat bumped alongside a small wooden pier and he climbed out. Paying the driver a reasonable amount of five hundred baht he stepped off the pier, and was confronted with a high rock face formation off to one side. Walking along the inclined uneven path, he reached a covered area with a makeshift canvas-style plastic roof, which offered shelter from the sun.

Some Buddhist monks were sitting at a wooden table there, whiling away the time. Some were reading newspapers or magazines. Others were busy staring at their mobile phones. Inwardly he smiled with mild surprise. Though he shouldn't have been surprised, on reflection. It seemed that no one was immune to modern technology.

A few metres further up Mark saw a solitary monk sitting at a desk under another makeshift canvas roof. The monk was selling tickets for entry to the temple. Mark bought one and the monk gestured him to continue further up.

He did so, and the path became steeper and less defined as he climbed. The final steps finished abruptly at a small flat rock platform no more than a few square feet in size. Black rusty railings alongside steep steps led sharply down into a large dark opening, which disappeared into the rock face.

After carefully descending the tricky staircase he walked through the entrance at the bottom, which opened up into a large cavern. He estimated the cavern to be a good 150 feet wide at least, and just short of that in depth. In the centre, running along the back wall, was a large golden Buddha statue lying on its side in a relaxed pose. In front was a large thin reddish patterned rug lying on the cavern floor for people to kneel on and pray. Numerous lit candles interspaced with flowers sat along the length of the Buddha. Incense wafted up, spreading its strong but gentle aroma.

A monk sat at a small desk inside selling incense, candles and flowers so people could use them for their prayers and offerings. Candles were lit everywhere and low-powered electric light bulbs were scattered about, illuminating the area.

As he took in the scene Mark felt uneasy. The energy was not good. It felt negative and oppressive. Unfriendly and dark. He wondered how people could not feel it while they were praying. How could the monks not feel it?

After walking over to the Buddha and then around the cave he saw a natural archway exiting the other side of the cavern, and walked over to it. A relatively narrow rock-walled passageway, enough for only two people to walk along at a time, led into another, slightly smaller natural cavern. This was also well lit. An altar to one side had a smaller Buddha, sitting cross-legged in the traditional pose.

As he looked around he saw there was another opening, which led down a small narrow natural corridor. Mark stepped in, his wide shoulders almost touching the walls and his head only a foot or so below the ceiling. Feeling claustrophobic, he continued down the long corridor for some minutes. His unease grew with each passing step and an unnatural feeling of frustration and anger built up within him. The corridor finally finished, opening up into yet another smaller cavern, some fifteen feet deep by ten feet wide.

Stepping inside he looked around and immediately sensed an evil presence. A black, old-fashioned rusty birdcage sat alone in an alcove. It looked like something from the 1920s, and ancient bird droppings and feathers littered the interior. Dark negative energy pulsated from within, making the atmosphere feel sick and hostile inside the whole cavern. It was almost typical of what you might see on the film set of a horror movie. There was something very wrong here, and Mark found his anger unnaturally growing by the second.

While staring at the cage intently from across the room he decided it was time to leave.

As he turned to depart a huge black form silently materialised, rising up out of the ground behind him. Roughly six feet tall and vaguely humanoid in shape, it seemed to blur slightly when looked at directly, as though you couldn't quite bring it into focus. A black glowing head sat upon its torso and two black eyes glittered with undisguised malice at his retreating back. Dark energy surrounded it, emanating in waves, making a sharp contrast to the dim light within the room.

Mark stopped mid step. Sensing imminent danger, he slowly turned. Energetic power automatically filled his body and surrounded him with white light, his defences immediately slamming into place.

Suddenly streams of large black crow-like birds flew like arrows directly at him from the previously empty cage. Anger coursed through him, and his hand swept across their path. Light beams of great power spat out destructive energy and obliterated the birds mid flight.

While turning his attention back to the demon in front of him, their eyes locked. Unmoving, they assessed each other.

Without warning, the demon leapt straight at him, its eyes glittering in triumph as dark energy streamed from its claw-like hands towards him. Had anyone else been facing it they would have been instantly overwhelmed.

But they weren't facing it. Mark was. And he was angry. The extending dark energy bounced off his shield, slipping past him harmlessly in dark, crackling waves.

Instantaneously two light guardians came to Mark's side, providing a tangible physical barrier in front of him. The demon's headlong rush was stopped dead in its tracks, and the guardians threw the demon back towards the other side of the room.

Surprised at their sudden appearance, the demon took stock for a moment. With eyes narrowing, it flung itself back at Mark's shield again. Raising his hands, white light punishingly slammed the demon back as it desperately clawed and struggled to reach him. Screaming its frustration and anger, it struggled violently, throwing out dark energy and smashing its body against the immovable force holding it back at the opposite wall.

After a few seconds the demon stood still, uncertain, robbed of its perceived easy prey.

But Mark's fury was barely contained. It had been building up ever since he entered the temple and he had now had enough.

'Is that all you've got?' he said in a deadly tone. 'You do it like this, demon.'

Raising his hands, his pent-up anger ripped out. Bright white light shot out of his hands across the cavern and struck the demon full in the chest with incredible force. There was a second's pause where time almost stood still. And the demon exploded. Its entire being shattering into a million fragments of light.

Mark watched as the fragments scattered and floated throughout the cavern, slowly disappearing without trace.

An unnatural silence ensued and Mark dropped his hands. Shocked at what he had just done, the urge to leave this vile place was strong within him. He turned around and followed yet more narrow pathways and caverns without incident till at last he came to some steps leading up. Light was visible above and he eagerly ascended, finally reaching the outside and sunlight.

Taking a deep breath he walked down the path, glancing at the oblivious Buddhist monks carrying on with their daily routines. On reaching the waiting boat he climbed in and sat down, and the helmsman immediately pushed off to start the return journey to his hotel.

His anger soon dissipated and Mark tried to gather his thoughts. What had just happened? Unable to obtain all the answers he wanted, he leant back, slowly recovering from the onslaught of adrenaline he had received only minutes ago, calming himself till he finally reached the pier and the relative safety of his hotel.

Author's Note

Being a member of any religion, be it Christian, Jewish, Muslim, Sikh, Hindu, Catholic, Buddhist, Spiritual or anything else, does not make you energetically aware or evolved. Or even a good person. What makes a good person comes from within. Not the label you place upon yourself.

Chapter 22

Reflection

That evening, having had his fill of food, Mark sat in a beer bar along a busy stretch of bars, clubs and restaurants that were the hub of the town's nightlife, quietly nursing a drink and mulling over what had occurred. First, he had done something that he had previously not known he could do. He had effectively obliterated the demon. Totally obliterated it. Bursting it into fragments, which had then just disappeared. Where had that come from? He had done something similar before, but not like that. He could have just used his own demon lords. Or sent the demon back down to the underworld. But no, he hadn't. He had obliterated it.

Thinking about it, he realised that it hadn't become nothing, as it were. It had exploded into fragments of light, which then floated away and disappeared. Had they reverted to light, maybe? It was an interesting concept.

Secondly … how could those monks know nothing about what was going on in their own temple? It almost defied belief. They should have been aware of the negative energies and dark forces within their own temple. And the people who visited and prayed? How could they not feel it, the very real danger they could be in?

In that moment a vast presence brushed his mind and spoke.

'So what is the lesson you have learnt today?'

Mark knew it was the spirit of Thailand speaking to him again.

'I have learnt that just because you are a monk or anything else, it is just a label. Those monks are following a path that looks as though they should know about these things. But they don't.'

'Exactly. You have learnt a valuable lesson. Just because you call yourself something, whatever it is, being spiritual, Hindu, Muslim, shamanic, a Buddhist monk, or anything else, does not mean that you are aware or can see or do the things you do. It is just a label. What makes a person good comes from the heart. Not the label they put upon themselves.'

There was a pause as Mark allowed this to sink in. Then the presence vanished.

As he sat there Mark knew it was true. He had known it before, but needed the experience to fully understand at a deeper level. Often this is the way. You can understand and know something intellectually, through learning. But you never really understand something, fully, completely, till you experience it yourself.

Relaxed and tired, he took a long swallow of his drink. His awareness tingled and he felt a negative energy coalescing behind him. Surreptitiously he turned his head and causally looked at the pool table behind him, which was now free of patrons. Standing on top of the pool table, right in the centre and in plain sight, was another demon. Roughly six feet in height, it crouched down slightly, its blackness in stark contrast to the brightly lit surroundings.

Mark knew it was common in areas such as bars and clubs, where emotions run high, for dark entities to be attracted to them. People drinking and getting intoxicated, sometimes using drugs and experiencing high emotions, anger, sex, anxiety, stress…all this leaves them vulnerable to dark forces, which feed off their light and spread negative energy and chaos as they see fit. The patrons of these places often, although unwittingly, serve the cause of darkness.

But why was the demon here, right behind him, when Mark was here at this time? This was no coincidence. Looking about he saw there were several customers sitting at the bar, and at other small bars close by. He had to be careful. The demon couldn't be allowed to run amok, and he couldn't be seen to be doing anything appearing too weird. They'd look at him as though he was crazy.

Keeping up the facade that he was unaware the demon was there and that his defences were down and he was vulnerable, he returned his gaze to the bar.

Closing his eyes his spirit left his body and immediately appeared on the pool table opposite the surprised demon.

Standing in his power, Mark's spirit shone brilliant white, and two white spirit soldiers appeared either side of him. But he didn't need them. Beams of light shot from his hands and wrapped themselves around the demon's arms, holding it fast.

'What do you want? Who are you?' he asked.

The demon remained silent and Mark squeezed his bonds tighter. The light burnt into its arms causing considerable pain.

He sensed the answer, and almost picked out the demon's thoughts without it saying anything.

It called itself a messenger and it was there to observe. To attack if the opportunity presented itself. Or just assess the situation. Its job was fluid. But it was there primarily to gain information. Then report back to its master.

When it had seen him drinking, apparently relaxed and off guard, it had thought he was vulnerable, so had showed itself ready to attack, striking him down if possible, disabling or weakening him if not. There would be a big reward for that.

Receiving his answer, Mark raised his arms and light shot out from his hands, streaming into the demon's chest. There was a moment's pause, and it exploded, scattering into a million fragments of light.

Re-entering his body Mark looked around. No one was taking any notice of him. His powers had grown and they now knew it. Their attacks had failed.

Sitting up straight he mentally spoke out to the powers that be, projecting his spirit voice across the ether.

'Take that message back to your master.'

And they heard him…

Chapter 23

England
The Coffee Shop

Mark had been back in the UK now for some weeks. Things had quietened down, and he was having a routine day. It was a busy morning with clients, then relaxing by himself in the gym. He had driven to his nearest town in Surrey to visit his local coffee shop and write some notes about his work for the remainder of the afternoon. After ordering a coffee and cake (the latter he allowed himself sometimes, the former often), he sat down and opened his laptop to write.

As he glanced up he noticed various people walking in. He enjoyed people watching, as most of us do. While slowly drinking his coffee he continued writing until he noticed a presence sitting at a table to his right. He glanced up and noticed a white male of medium build and short dark hair sitting down at the table next to him some five feet away.

Something didn't feel quite right, and as he looked up and caught his eye the man spoke to him.

'Hello, how are you?'

Busy writing and not wishing to be disturbed, Mark answered politely.

'I'm good, thank you,' and continued typing.

'You're not watching the royal wedding, then?' the man continued.

'No,' Mark replied, turning his head and carrying on writing. Something was not right, and Mark trusted his instincts. The man appeared to be mentally ill in some way. Mark had had considerable experience in dealing with such people. But there was something else.

As he continued to write the man carried on saying random things. Mark grunted his reply and carried on writing. Eventually he realised that Mark wasn't going to answer and started talking to himself, making occasional burping noises while he did so.

Soon Mark could feel negative energy coming towards him, emanating from the man with increasing strength. He closed himself down instantly and erected a barrier between him and the man to block it. The negative energy had a very dark feel to it, and Mark bolstered the shield with a spirit guide on each side reinforcing it.

Having established an effective block against the dark energy, he reached out with his senses to feel for the exact source.

A dark energy form, standing behind the man to his right, began to take shape. It was a demon. No wonder the man seemed mentally unstable. He had no chance with this demon influencing him constantly.

Mark looked around the coffee shop. People were busy doing their own thing and it was only half-full. But still, they would soon notice if someone started acting strangely. Add to that all the varied energies that were rampant in there, with the constant flow of people…the situation was far from ideal for him to deal with it.

But he had no choice. Nor would he turn away from his duty. It was one of those many situations that he had to deal with for the greater good.

After mulling the problem over for a few seconds he closed his eyes and prepared to step out of his body to confront the demon.

Almost immediately he felt physically uncomfortable, and did not like his eyes being closed. Closing off your physical senses makes it easier to use your alternative non-physical senses, but in these circumstances it would draw unwanted attention.

He decided to try something else. Opening his eyes he stared at his laptop and allowed his eyes to unfocus, gazing unseeingly at the screen. This helped him enter a state of non-being and leave his physicality behind.

Mark stepped out of his body, aware of his physical body sitting behind him staring at the laptop, to all intents and purposes just reading. No one would be any the wiser.

Satisfied, he walked past his shield and stood in front of the demon. A black silhouette in generic human form with a body, head, arms and legs was all he could make out. Dark energy pulsated from it and he knew instantly that no questions were needed. This one was just pure evil, and Mark didn't have the time in this situation to play around. You can't mess around with these things, and sometimes you have to take immediate action for everyone's safety.

Focusing himself and his power, Mark stepped in closer. Then, raising both arms with clenched fists, he slammed them down on top of the demon and drove it towards the floor. Shocked by the suddenness and ferocity of the attack, the demon floundered. Following through, he stamped on its body, attempting to drive it straight back into the underworld whence it came. The demon appeared to sink down under his blows. But it wasn't enough.

Trying to recover, it started to rise and fight back.

Knowing this had to be dealt with swiftly, Mark focused and opened up a portal directly below the demon, and with several terrifying blows he slammed the demon down through the portal back into the inky depths of the underworld below.

With a wave of his hand the portal slammed shut, barring any chance of its return.

Mark surveyed the area, making sure it had gone before stepping back into his body. He opened his physical eyes and refocused, taking a moment to bring his physical awareness back into sync. Surreptitiously he glanced across at the table to his right. No sign of the demon could be seen. Checking the energies around him he could tell that the dark negative force hitting his barrier had stopped, and nodded inwardly with satisfaction.

He turned his head slightly and looked at the man, who in turn was already staring at him. A strange look was in his eyes but he said nothing. Keeping his shield in place, Mark relaxed slightly. While no demon was attacking him now or influencing the man, he was still clearly not in a good place.

Five minutes later, and still talking to himself, the man got up and walked over to the exit, where he stopped and hung around for several minutes, still talking to himself and staring at Mark. Mark knew that the best way to avoid this unwanted situation was to make no eye contact or engage verbally with him, and after a few minutes the man left the coffee shop.

Taking a breath he relaxed. It was not the best place for dealing with such things, yet it had had to be done. There was a bigger picture, as always. And Mark knew he served the greater good and was not about just helping paying clients.

Very few would ever know everything that he did. But that's the way of things, and he was happy to pay the price for his abilities. And, if not him, then who else? Should he have left the man to the influence and disruption of the demon? No, the demon had to be dealt with so it could cause no more harm to him or anyone else. And at least the man now had a chance.

Mark realised something in that moment. There was a time when an experience like that would have drained him significantly. But not this time. Not at all.

A sense of quiet satisfaction came over him. He had further grown in power. Silently acknowledging this, he turned his attention back to his book.

Chapter 24

The Messenger

Mark often attended well-being and spiritual events, and on one particular day he was doing exactly that in an affluent town in southern England. Having a stand at such events helped him to connect with people and offer short sessions of healing and life guidance. He found this was one of the most effective ways of connecting with a greater number of people. He could increase their knowledge and awareness, heal many, and give people the chance to speak and connect with him.

Often he found that some had been waiting for this event 'knowing' they were going to see him. Or had actually been 'informed' by spirit that he would be there at this location and time. Some people actually said they had been waiting for years to see him and had been given only his name, or that someone there would be able to help them with their unique problem.

It was a humbling thought.

The events tended to run all day, and Mark thoroughly enjoyed these days. On this particular day he was very focused. It is not easy to constantly tune into different people, scenarios and energies throughout the day, so you really have to be on the ball so to speak.

Every single person comes to you with a problem, and by default some form of negative energy. That is not to say it is generally dangerous. It is not. That's rare. But the constant switching from one energy to the next, controlling the energies involved, protecting yourself, and tuning into each individual you connect with, is draining and requires constant focus. Of course, in certain scenarios it could be dangerous, depending on what was involved. But fortunately the more difficult clients with their various problems invariably gravitate towards the person who can help them.

Mark was in good spirits as he dealt with his first few clients, and it was while giving a healing session halfway through the morning that his attention was drawn to a suspicious-looking white male wandering around. Tall and slim, with a pasty complexion, he had slightly stooped shoulders and lank black hair, and a somewhat sly look on his face.

Mark's eyes passed over him and immediately flicked away, but he continued to observe him surreptitiously as the man loitered in the background. He was making a show of looking at the variety of stands and whatever random items took his eye. But Mark knew he wasn't genuinely looking. His eyes never really focused on the apparent object of interest.

Something just seemed off. He kept wandering over to Mark's table and hanging around while Mark himself was talking to various individuals.

Mark was well versed in how to avoid contact with people he didn't wish to connect with and avoided all eye contact, keeping himself visibly busy with others and apparently unavailable. Eventually, apparently bored with waiting, the man reluctantly wandered off.

Instinctively Mark knew something was very wrong. His spider sense, as he often described it when talking about it to others, was sounding off in a big way. This man was dark. Dark, intelligent, and a potential threat. He didn't know how exactly. But he was.

An hour or so later, while speaking to another member of the public, the man appeared again, hovering in the background. He was looking for his moment, and seemingly determined on waiting to speak to him now. Eventually Mark's clients left, and he realised the inevitability of having to speak to him.

The man approached with a slightly lopsided tilt to his head and looked at him out of the side of his eye. Wary, Mark offered a slight smile in return. His defences had sprung up immediately, sliding smoothly into place.

The man started speaking and rambled on, with generic greetings in the mix. Mark wasn't paying too much attention to what he was saying because his mind was on the more important aspects of what might really be going on.

The seconds dragged by and then he heard the word 'demonologist'. His ears perked up and, tuning back into the conversation, he refocused on what the man was saying to him.

'Mark,' he continued, 'I see you do what I do. I deal with demons also.'

'Really?' Mark said politely. 'You do what I do? What do you do, then?'

'I'm a demonologist.'

'Uh-huh,' Mark replied noncommittally.

'Yes, I've been doing it for decades,' he said fervently.

Mark looked at him. He could be no more than in his mid to late thirties. Looking for a way to avoid as much contact with him as possible Mark replied cautiously,

'I see. That's interesting.'

'My name's Peter, by the way,' he said, offering his hand. Mark shook it. It was limp and clammy to the touch. Shaking it firmly, Mark resisted recoiling from the damp, cold flesh.

Peter continued to talk about his work with demons and clearing houses.

'I've been doing this for decades,' he continued to say, talking to him as though he was a comrade in arms and they could be best friends.

Mark just listened and watched, murmuring,

'I see,' in the intervals where appropriate.

Peter's manner and conversation became oilier and oilier as the words continued to flow. And Mark's discomfort grew. He was all but shuddering inwardly at this person's mannerisms and energy.

Having had enough of his toxic presence, he decided to change tack. Skilfully manipulating a way to close the conversation and get away from him, Mark spoke in reply, turning it away from its current course.

'Perhaps it's time for you to have a stand yourself here. Why have you not done so?'

The dark energy which Mark noticed earlier coalesced around him, gently oozing from his aura.

Hissing, he replied,

'Perhaps I will. I just haven't got round to it yet. Who do I speak to?'

'Just go upstairs,' Mark replied, pointing off to the left. 'There are officials up there who will give you the details you need.'

The man paused, thinking for a moment, obviously looking for a way out of Mark's closing parry. Mark said nothing as he subtly slid into place an energetic shield between them, an impenetrable wall of light.

Black tendrils slowly extended towards Mark as the man's energy shifted, stopping as they touched the shield. Probing. Tentatively they withdrew. Mark gave no signal that he had been aware of the energetic exchange.

As the seconds passed, and with the silence between them extending, Peter, as he called himself, realised that the meeting was drawing to a close and struggled to find a way of continuing. Mark stayed silent and impassive, finally forcing him to speak.

'Thank you. Perhaps I'll do that. Here is my card.'

He offered his business card to Mark, who took it carefully by the edges between thumb and forefinger and placed it on the table in front of him.

'Thanks,' he replied, making no further attempt at conversation. He was just anxious to be rid of him.

The man known as Peter took a step back.

'Nice to speak to you,' he said with a slight smile.

'And to you,' Mark replied.

The man offered his hand and Mark shook it briefly. The man's hand was moist and clammy still, and Mark let go as swiftly as politeness allowed.

The man turned away and walked off towards the stairs. Mark turned to the side and took a deep breath of relief. Then immediately turned back around and looked in the direction he had walked. The walkway was empty. Quickly he scanned the area. The stairs were some twenty metres away and also empty. There were no exits or doors. There were just a few people walking around the stalls on the sides of the hall. His line of vision was completely clear wherever he looked. Yet there was no trace of him. He had simply vanished. In literally a couple of seconds. There was no way he could have done that, just disappear out of sight in that time. None. It just wasn't possible.

And yet, somehow, he had.

A sense of disquiet and confusion flowed through Mark. He knew he could have dealt with him, but there's a time and place. And now was not the time or the place.

With his thumb and forefinger Mark carefully picked up the card sitting on his desk. The energy in the card was sick. Holding it by the edges to minimise contact, he walked into the public toilets behind him and dropped the card straight in the bin. Then he washed his hands thoroughly in the sink behind to clear the sick energy from holding the card and shaking the man's hand. Swiftly he called down light though his entire body, washing himself clean of any link and residue of dark energy attached to him from his encounter.

Mark pondered for a moment. At these public events there are usually quite a number of people needing help with some kind of problem or another. It's to be expected. And by default they will have negative energy around them. That's just the way it is. These people are drawn to the light and potential healing, and the help that comes within these wellness events. It's one of the purposes these events serve.

The vast majority of people who attend them are genuine. But some are not. Dark ones can also be attracted to the light, feeding off the positive energy as well as the negative carried by some. But this man was something different. Different to the normal comings and goings of dark and light beings.

Mark put him to the back of his mind, as the clients milled around him. But he didn't forget.

The day went ahead as usual, and Mark met many good decent people and clients, with lots of new people drawn into his sphere of influence.

Towards the latter half of the day the steady flow of people wishing to see him continued unabated, and Mark was forced to turn some of them away. He always tried to see as many as possible, but this was the usual scenario at the well-being events he attended. His appointment slots always booked up so fast, that by early to mid afternoon at the latest he was fully booked and having to turn people away.

After packing his belongings neatly away and stowing them into the back of his car he took his leave and drove home. The weather was wet and cold and Mark tried to switch off and relax without very much success.

Author's Note

We live in a world of energy. This energy interacts. After being in the presence of a sick person or environment some of that energy could then stick to you. After being in contact with some form of negative energy you should always wash your hands. Or, even better, shower if possible. For more heavy exposure a salt bath might be more appropriate.

This, of course, doesn't fix everything. But it does help, and in lesser cases is often sufficient. The element of water removes the negative or sick energy. As a healer or therapist, never place your hands back on your body till you have washed them. You've just removed and immersed your hands in sick energy. Why would you want that to be transmitted back into you? Which it will, by default.

Think of it as if you have put your hands in mud. Then you place your hands on your nice clean clothing. The mud will transfer from the contact. It's the same thing. So, after being in contact with any negative energy, or healing a client if you are a therapist, wash your hands immediately afterwards.

This is why a therapist, after healing or helping you, will often not have any bodily contact with you due to the exchange of energies.

CHAPTER 25

RA

As soon as Mark walked into his house an hour later, he went to the bathroom to run himself a salt bath to cleanse some of the negative energy he had no doubt accumulated over the day.

While pottering around upstairs waiting for the bath to fill he sensed a presence. Pausing for a moment he extended his senses, and almost immediately knew exactly who it was. The man from the well-being event. Peter. Seeing him for the first time in his mind's eye, he recognised him for the dark, controlled being he was. He had invaded his home, his stronghold, and that was both bold and a direct challenge. Mark knew he had to deal with it.

Behaving as though he had not noticed the threat, he causally moved across to the landing and sat on the edge of the stairs. Settling himself down in a relaxed manner he closed his eyes. To the eyes of an outsider it would appear as though he was just chilling and about to meditate. Focusing, he grounded himself through the base of his spine and his feet, delving deep into the earth.

Surreptitiously he called in his spirit guides and four angels, one for each corner, who swiftly formed a protective grid around him. A large powerful light warrior appeared alongside also. Prepared, he released his spirit and travelled to where he felt Peter to be, and immediately found himself in a zone that could only be described as the middle of nowhere, a limitless grey void of nothingness. Everything was grey and totally devoid of anything as far as you could see or feel.

Extending his senses outwards he scanned the area, and moments later was rewarded as he detected Peter's presence in the distance somewhere ahead. In spirit form he moved within the void, heading towards where he felt him to be, constantly scanning his surroundings. After what seemed only a short space of time, but in reality could have been any span of time or distance, he stood before the spirit form of Peter.[***]

Looking at him through spirit eyes Mark could see there was no doubt he worked for darkness. His essence was totally filled with dark matter. Although he walked the physical plane in human form he was infused with dark energy, controlled by forces from the underworld, and could no longer be called human.

Even though this being was more darkness than human he instinctively knew he shouldn't use darkness to fight darkness. Mark glowed white as he infused himself with light. Flanked by his guides and guardians he stood fully in his power.

'You will leave me alone,' he commanded. 'And you will go.'

*** When you are travelling within the non physical realms, regardless of what realm it is, time and distance are completely different and almost have no meaning in comparison to the physical world. This is demonstrated even within a basic meditation where you will often sense a complete lack of time elapsing, and at the end of the meditation wonder where the last half hour has gone as it felt like only a few minutes. This is because you let go of the physical and enter the energetic/spirit realm, so normal times, feelings and distances no longer apply whilst there.

The being known as Peter looked at him, its energy intensifying and becoming darker and denser. Malice emanated from it in waves.

Staring at the being in front of him, Mark repeated his command with more power.

'You will leave me alone.'

The dark one stood still, staring back. And said nothing. Its dark energy convulsed and weaved, edging towards him. Mark didn't move. Assessing each other's power, the two light and dark forms faced off.

Mark knew instantly that his regular guides were not going to be enough. Thinking quickly, the image of a powerful golden form sprang into his thoughts. Ra. Although he had been known by other names long forgotten with the passage of time, most people in this millennium knew him as Ra. The Egyptian Sun god. Worshipped thousands of years ago, he was a deity in his own right.

His huge form appeared at Mark's side. But it wasn't so much his physical size that made him so impressive, though he could be as big as a country mansion, or bigger if he so wished. It was the sheer power that emanated from within, the arrogance and confidence he literally oozed. Glowing a deep brilliant orange, almost like the sun itself, Ra's power was immense. He exuded the energy and the belief in his divine right to rule and be obeyed. And nobody could mistake him for exactly who and what he was. Ra, god of the Sun. And he knew it.

Uncertainty now clouding its features, the dark one looked at the new arrival. The situation had changed drastically and the balance of power had shifted. Massively outgunned, it hesitated. No longer so confident, its own arrogance still wouldn't allow it to be so easily intimidated.

Mark repeated his command.

'You will leave. You will not attack me. You will not harm anyone connected with me or under my protection. My family, my loved ones or my friends. Nor anyone else in any way connected to me.'

Still not completely cowed, the dark one stood there, momentarily pensive. Whether it was due to false bravado, bluff or sheer stupidity, he didn't know and didn't care.

Without hesitating, Mark gave a silent nod. And Ra struck with the speed of thought. A wall of impenetrable brilliant white light surrounded the dark one, wrapping around it like a cocoon and lifting it several metres off the floor with its feet dangling. Momentarily shocked, it beat ineffectively against the constricting barrier in a mixture of rage and fear.

Ra stared at the helpless dark form in front of him as its arms were violently flung out and legs slammed together, forming a crucifix. The crucifix cocoon turned a deep bright orange, matching the colour of its captor.

Shaking and roaring its dismay, the dark one struggled desperately against its bonds. Then Ra set him on fire.

This was the fire of a god, and the dark one screamed in agony. In desperation it slipped into its true form. The outer energy slipping away to reveal the demon beneath. The now visible demon made a desperate lurch towards the void just outside, and beckoning freedom from the flames of Ra. But it was futile.

Failing to escape it turned its head screaming, and then its scream took on a different note, one tinged with victory through its pain.

Mark's sixth sense stood on end and he instantly spun round. Beings of darkness appeared from within the void and raced towards him. Bright white light shot out of his hands, slicing through their ranks and cutting through them like a knife through butter. More beings appeared and were blasted into oblivion as they did so. Their heads disappeared as brilliant white light struck them, and the rest of them vanished moments later.

Ra's fire intensified till the demon was completely incapacitated. Held fast by his bonds, no longer able to even scream in agony, it could do nothing but burn.

Mark stepped forward and spoke.

'You will leave here, never to return. You will not come near me or anyone I know again. Come against me or anyone under my protection, my family, or anyone I know and I will destroy you. Utterly.'

Unable to answer, it was totally helpless against the power of Ra.

Mark waited and watched it burn. Seconds passed till its acquiescence slid through the demon's agony.

With a nod, and a gesture of acknowledgement to Ra, Mark vanished from the void and returned to his body, leaving the demon to its fate.

Sitting once again within his physical body, he looked via his mind's eye and saw the demon still being held, the flames burning so brightly he could barely look. And still it burnt.

Mark knew that it would stay there, trapped in the void in never-ending burning agony, till the powers that be, and Ra, deemed that it should be released.

Taking a deep breath Mark withdrew his consciousness from the scene. Settling his physical form fully back to Earth he took a moment to ground himself, extending his senses to check his surroundings.

The danger was over, and Mark thought for a moment about what had happened. He was able to make sense of it. They had changed their tactics. This man was a messenger from the dark side who had been sent to entice him to their side or, failing that, to destroy him.

They had failed. Fortunately. But it was a sober reminder to him to be on his guard at all times, as the darkness would always be there. Spreading mayhem. Coercing where they could, or destroying where they couldn't. And he was on their radar.

Taking in a breath of satisfaction, Mark acknowledged that he had won this battle. It had been a severe blow to the dark side. For now. And it would be a while before they tried again.

Author's Note

Ra

Ra is known as the Sun god by most in modern times (for the last few thousand years, at any rate). And, for reasons Mark had never fully understood, Ra had taken an interest in him from very early on in his training. In his first spiritual development group with his original teacher Ra had appeared mid session while he had been practising channelling spirit.

Mark remembered very clearly that first meeting. He was sitting in circle with the group, and practising connecting to spirit. The seconds went by, and slowly something started to connect with him. It was heavy and strong. As that sensation increased he felt an enormous presence come forward, threatening to engulf him and take over. While struggling to maintain his sense of identity, a very literal feeling of great weight seemed to drive him into the ground. His head spun as though he was on drugs, and he lost all sense of reality and control of his body.

Desperately he pushed back and drove his roots deep into the earth to become more grounded, and slowly regained some control over his mind and body. He was scared at the time, and said so. But his teacher had recognised who it was and reassured the inexperienced Mark.

'It's only because you are so strong that he has come through,' she said. 'He wouldn't do that with anyone else here. He chose you because you have that strength.'

Reassured, Mark had allowed the connection, enabling Ra to use his body as a vessel and talk through him, while he strained and succeeded, just, to keep a sense of self and control.

There followed a most bizarre conversation between the teacher and Ra/Mark, and though he shared some of Ra's emotions and could fully hear the exchange, he felt like a bystander witnessing one of the strangest conversations he'd ever been privy to.

Linked as they were, he could feel Ra's humour in the situation and his not unkind arrogance. But arrogance it was. He had a divine belief in his right to rule and to demand being acknowledged as a god. The whole experience was both scary and surreal.

When Ra was finished he acknowledged Mark directly. This was an acknowledgement of Mark's strength in standing up to him and his ability of being his vessel.

As the years went by he received sporadic visits from Ra. Sometimes he would test Mark, and by default train him. Occasionally he deigned to help him, appearing when he chose at the most unexpected and unanticipated times. As the years went by and Mark's abilities and strength grew, the visits had become more frequent, and a respectful alliance was formed whereby Mark could on occasion call him. If he chose, he would appear and assist.

What he knew for sure was that somehow they had a connection. Ra was a kindred spirit, almost, and they had an understanding and a mutual respect for one another.

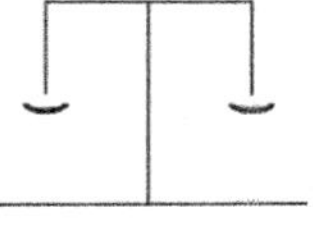

Chapter 26

Native American

The following morning Mark received a text message from a friend and fellow light worker, Chloe, saying that she had recommended a client of hers should see him. It was a long text and he read through it carefully.

She had treated this female client a couple of times and done some work with her, but she now required something else. She had completed some rudimentary clearing of her energies and removed a couple of attachments, this in turn had revealed something potentially much deeper, and she felt she was no longer the right person for the job. She had also sensed other beings in the background but was unable to deal with them.

There was a lot of darkness surrounding this woman, and she knew instinctively that she wasn't the person to deal with it. Apparently over the years this woman had seen many different healers of reputation and the problem had not been resolved.

One further concern was that during the healing session she had broken into talking in a Native American language, very aggressively, gesticulating and contorting her face angrily, as though she was possessed. She was able to stop when asked, but claimed to not know any Native American language. She seemed totally genuine. On being questioned she stated she could feel what she believed was a Native American spirit take over and talk through her, using her body as a vessel.

Mark had known Chloe for many years and trusted what she was saying. It was an intriguing case and he was always willing to help. He picked up the phone and called her.

'Hey Chloe, it's Mark. How are you?'

'Good thanks. How are you?'

'Yes, all good, thanks. What's all this about? Sounds weird. Even for us.'

'I know. I've seen her a couple of times now. Worked on her energies, and found a couple of Native American attachments, which I managed to get rid of. But it seemed much deeper than that. And she started to talk in Native American. I managed to calm her down and and it stopped but I couldn't get any more from it.'

'Are you saying that she actually started speaking in a foreign language she doesn't know?' Mark asked.

'Yes. A Native American language. I did manage to calm her down, but it's gone beyond me. I don't think I'm the one to deal with this now. It's very dark. Apparently she has seen several healers over the years, including those who deal with spirit removal who said they could help, but nothing has ever worked and the problems have never gone away.'

'Hmm. That is strange. OK, I'll see her. What's her name? Have you given her my details?'

'Yes. She'll definitely call you. Her name's Francesca. By the way, she's also spiritual and been training for some time, under a couple of teachers we know. They were not able to resolve the problem either,' Chloe replied.

'OK, that's interesting. Leave it with me and I'll let you know what happens. Thanks.'

Mark put the phone down. This did sound very interesting, he thought. He had a moment of wondering whether she would call or not. But something inside told him she would.

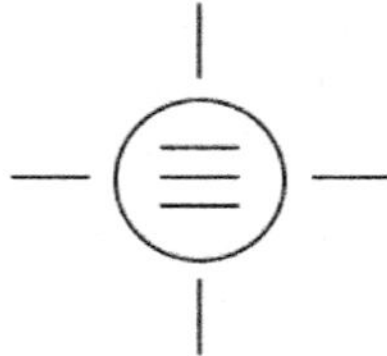

CHAPTER 27

THE LIVING PORTAL

Within a few days Mark received an email from Francesca and an appointment was made to see her the following week. That day quickly arrived.

Mark was sitting and preparing before her arrival. Feeling slightly on alert, he prepared himself accordingly while waiting for her to knock on the door.

He stood upstairs by the window to gain a view of her arrival prior to her actually knocking on the door. Sometimes he found it useful to observe clients for a few seconds as they got out of their cars and walked up the path. It gave him vital seconds to gather information and assess the situation.

Today was no exception as Francesca pulled up and parked on the drive. As she stepped out of the car wearing jeans and a loose-fitting cotton top he could see that she was a tall, slim woman with a commanding manner. Short dark hair framed attractive features, and Mark gauged her to be around forty-five. But, looking beyond the physical, she appeared energetically unbalanced... It was more than that. Something wasn't right.

With a calming breath, grounding and shielding himself, he

walked downstairs and opened the door to greet her.

'Hi, Francesca. Come in.'

'Thanks,' she replied, stepping through the door as Mark moved back to allow her in.

Immediately he felt something was wrong. She smiled on the outside, but inside she was tense.

After pouring her a glass of water he gestured for her to enter the lounge where he greeted clients. Following her in he took a seat opposite the sofa where she was sitting.

He sat back and took a few moments to assess her, his gaze taking in her energy and general manner. Though he sensed she was indeed a strong, confident woman, she was ill at ease.

Mark spoke, seeking to help her relax.

'How was your journey?

'Good, thanks. It didn't take me long,' she replied.

'Good. Glad to hear it. How are you feeling?'

'Not bad, thanks. OK.'

'So why are you here, then?' Mark replied with a smile and humour in his eyes.

She returned the smile and relaxed.

She sat back and reached for a notebook next to her with well-thumbed pages and Post-it notes sticking out between them.

Taking her time she answered.

'It's a long story.'

'We have time,' he replied, settling down.

Francesca launched into a fascinating tale which started about ten years ago when she first began her spiritual development, which involved following a path she had always felt was right for her. She attended a spiritual development circle, gradually evolving and developing herself, though not as fast as she would have liked. Sometimes she also struggled to connect with the teacher.

As she developed she felt a Native American spiritual influence grow within her, which was sometimes troubling, but she kept it under control. She mentioned it to her teacher, who helped and advised her. But it always seemed to keep intruding, though at a manageable level. However, as she developed her abilities and connection further, the presence seemed to grow accordingly.

'Then they started to talk through me,' she continued. 'They made me feel bad and took over my personality. They would wake me up at night. And I would feel the urge to talk in another language and experience pains in my body.'

Listening intently Mark spoke, trying to get the full picture.

'So you started going to a development group about ten years ago?'

'Yes,' she replied. 'But I didn't really get any real problems till about three or four years ago. I've seen various healers, and they couldn't do anything. They told me certain things and told me they had removed things and it was being dealt with. But nothing changed.'

'Who were these healers? Did they specialise in removing attachments and dark energy?' Mark asked.

'Yes.' She then named two or three healers who Mark had heard of.

'I know two of them, and they are good at their job. One of them in particular knows what he's doing with this kind of thing. What did he say?'

'Well, I saw him a couple of times. He removed some attachments from me and said he had called in a big spirit, which I can't remember the name of, and said it was being dealt with. I haven't managed to get hold of him since.'

'And it hasn't worked?'

'No. I still have the same problem and I've run out of people to ask. Then I met Chloe, who I saw a couple of times. She was great. Really helped. But she has now said I need to see you.'

'Yes, I have spoken to Chloe. She told me what has happened,' Mark replied.

'I'm desperate, Mark. I don't feel I'm Francesca any more. I've lost myself. It's taking me over and I don't know what to do. I have no one else to turn to. Chloe is the only one who I really felt understood what I was going through and actually helped.'

He could hear the desperation in her voice. She was afraid, disillusioned and had almost given up.

Mark paused for a moment then leant forward in his chair and looked at her intently.

'Don't worry. I'm sure I can help. Let's see what we can do. Have you ever meditated before?'

'Yes,' she replied. 'Many times. But I've always struggled, because of this Native American thing.'

Assessing the situation Mark made a decision.

'I think today we just need to start healing. Come over into the healing room and sit on the chair,' he said.

Author's Note

An attachment is a generic term for an energetic being literally attached to your person. This can be deep inside you or on the outer edges of your aura or anywhere in between. It can be a dark entity or a simple non intelligent life form such as a low level parasite. The term on occasion can also be used to refer to non living objects attached to your aura. For example devices, knives, cords, bindings and a multitude of others.

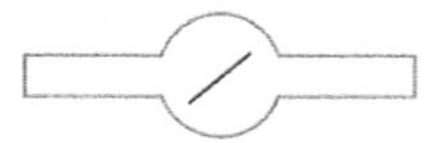

Chapter 28

Possession

The healing room was directly attached to Mark's lounge and was, in fact, a conservatory that had been converted into a full-time healing room. Two sides were made of glass, and, combined with the glass roof, they allowed a lot of natural light in, giving it an airy, open feel. The roof also had a heat-reflective coating on it, which helped to keep the room a comfortable temperature all year round. The overall effect was a well-lit room full of natural light, where you could look up at the sky when lying back on the therapy couch, and clients felt very relaxed there.

To one side was a five-foot table laden with a variety of beautiful crystals. On the other side, set at a thirty-degree angle, was a wide therapy couch covered with a red throw.

Between the table and the couch was a high-backed brown leather chair, which Mark gestured to Francesca to sit on. Many years of healing there had given the room a powerful, peaceful and healing energy, which everyone noticed.

Standing behind her, he spoke.

'Just relax and close your eyes.'

Grounding himself, Mark closed his own eyes and focused, encasing himself in a shield of white light and closing his chakras down. Checking all his usual guides were in situ, he placed his hands on either side of her head.

Feeling the energy exchange between his hands and Francesca's head he began to get a feel for where she was energetically, and could sense what was going on with the whole of her body, both inside and out. Mark placed himself in a complete state of awareness of everything around him.

Something different was going on here, he thought. Tuning in further, deepening his awareness, a Native American male presence appeared in the room. Hostile energies emitted from him and he wasn't happy.

Mark spoke out loud to him.

'What do you want?'

Waves of hostility was his answer.

Francesca spoke.

'He's very angry. He really doesn't like you.'

'I know,' Mark replied. 'That's normal, as he knows what I will do. But the question is …why is he here? Something else is going on here.'

Other Native American energies, coming from within, were evident inside Francesca. Mark had a sense of several of them. Not all hostile, but rather a mix of emotions.

Pushing the angry male to the side with a wave of his hand he connected with the others inside her, and placed his hand on her heart. Foremost was a female Native American, who was sad and very distressed. She just wanted to be released. Behind her he sensed others.

But there was no way he could deal with them while this large angry male was hanging around, getting more irate by the minute. Mark stepped back in front of her and concentrated his attention on him. Gazing intently, he focused, and with a wave of his hand the angry male disappeared.

Francesca's eyes were still closed, but her mouth was now twitching and her lips were moving erratically. Her jaw flexed from side to side as though something was aggravating her mouth and almost trying to take her over.

'He is going mad inside me. This is what happens. I can hear he wants to speak and I am trying to control it,' she said, struggling to keep her voice under control.

'OK, let him speak,' Mark replied, as he silently took a few steps back and to the side to observe.

There was a moment's transition, a small moment where you could see a change taking place.

Then Francesca's face twisted into a mask of rage as she let go. Her eyes still closed, and with an air of calculated malice, she slowly leant forward in the chair with an expression of utter contempt. Francesca/it paused for a second. Then her head turned violently in his direction, almost a full ninety degrees, and looked straight at him.

Mark was shocked. There was no way she knew where he was standing as her tightly screwed-up eyes bored into his. It could see him! Her face became a picture of pure fury as what sounded like Native American words poured out of her mouth, dripping venom and menace as she spat the words out with disdain.

On bare feet Mark silently walked across the front of her to the other side to move behind. As he did so Francesca's/its head turned with him, following his movement exactly, staring straight at him with eyes still screwed shut, spitting out obscenities. Although he couldn't understand the language, its intention and utter contempt were clear.

This woman was speaking in a foreign language unknown to her, and had followed his exact movements with her eyes shut tight. She/it could still see him. It was like something out of the film *The Exorcist.*

The tirade of obscenities continued as the spirit ranted at him with total contempt and extreme hostility, punctuating its words with facial gestures that spoke volumes, as much as the actual words. Her whole demeanour and body movements were no longer her own.

Standing in his power, Mark reinforced his defences.

Calmly he spoke.

'You are not wanted here. It is time for you to go.'

Its answer was direct and to the point. Despite his not understanding the words its meaning was very clear. Scorn marked every syllable it uttered.

Light beams streamed out of his hands, securing the spirit within. Instinctively he knew that he needed to find a different way of dealing with this. As his thought processes went out, a new spirit being came forth that he had been learning to work with that called itself a kind of cosmic soldier or mercenary for the greater good. Mark still had yet to explore the full potential of this cosmic being.

By allowing him to seamlessly blend in within his own energy, Mark found he could tap into its power and use his abilities. Fresh beams of light shot out of his hands with significantly enhanced strength, gripping the spirit without stepping any closer to Francesca. Standing several feet away, palms open, he raised his arms lifting the spirit up and out of her.

The usurper of Francesca's body dangled helplessly in his light bonds. Energetic cords still linked them and her face contorted as her body spasmed in reaction. With an effortless surge of power the spirit was punched like a projectile high into the sky, culminating in being held in impotent suspension mid-air.

For a moment Mark observed the tiny figure in the distance. It was so high up it looked like an Action Man toy. Its anger was still palpable, but it was unable to break free of its restraints. Shock and hostility emanated from it in equal measure.

Seconds later two spirit guards appeared, one either side of it, and took hold of its arms. Then the guards vanished, taking the foul entity with them.

As he dropped his arms Mark marvelled at what he had done. He had never done that before. He'd discovered a new ability using light, and it was powerful.

His cosmic soldier stepped out of him and Mark looked at Francesca, slumped in her chair.

'How do you feel?' he asked.

Tentatively she moved her mouth around, as though loosening her jaw muscles.

'Better. I think it's gone.'

'It has. We need to release the others now.'

He moved her on to the couch and she lay down gratefully on her back.

'I think there are more, you know.'

'I know,' he replied. 'We'll deal with them now.'

Placing his hands above her heart he focused on the energies there.

A female Native American came forward, clearly distressed.

Francesca started to sob.

'What's going on, Francesca?' he asked.

'It's the emotions of them. There is more than one. They are hysterical and scared.'

Reaching down and speaking in gentle tones, he gently eased the frightened female spirit out of the heart chakra.

'It's OK. You are safe now. You can go home.'

A shining white gateway appeared a few feet off to the side and above, glowing with invitation and peace. The spirit allowed Mark to assist her through the gateway, where she disappeared.

Another female Native American spirit appeared in the centre of her heart chakra. Speaking in the same soothing tones, he eased her into the gateway also. One after another came through. As each one did Mark gently pulled them out and then passed them over into the waiting gateway.

Spirit joined with him, and answers came with a knowing.

Francesca was being used as a portal. Many years ago in a previous life she had been a powerful Native American witch doctor, and that was where her deepest roots were, attached to that life. All these souls were using her as a gateway to freedom.

Mark allowed the monitoring spirit beings working alongside in the room to speak through him out loud.

'They have been trapped. You are a portal for all these Native Americans to be released. This is part of your path, and was agreed prior to you coming down in physical form again. The Native American you removed by force was holding them captive and blocking the way for them to cross over.'

Mark went quiet and the spirit beings did too. Sensing there was more, he asked, using his spirit voice,

'What's happening here?'

Speaking only to him, spirit answered.

'Francesca is a portal – a bridge, if you like – between realms for souls to cross over. Native American souls.'

'Why her?'

'She was a high priestess a very long time ago in a previous life, and wielded great power. She has a long history of being Native American within her. It's her core life, if you will. Even now she has great power just by being the portal. Some wish to control the portal and her because of this bridge that is used for the crossing of souls. With this control comes power. The control and feeding off souls. It is very similar in this physical world, with human trafficking, slavery, and gangs controlling people for their own ends.

'This spirit was holding her back. It is also connected to her soul group. They are a Native American soul group and jealous of her. They know who she is. Some love her. Some hate her. And now, even though she is no longer in that position and in that life, they want to hang on to her light and control her.'

That answered many questions, and Mark went silent for a moment.

The presence left him, and Mark glanced at Francesca. Tears were running down her cheeks and she was stifling small sobs.

'Are you OK?' he asked.

'It's the gratitude. All I can feel now is gratitude from them being released.'

'Well, it's OK now. We shall help some more cross over.'

For a half an hour Mark released soul after soul into the light, till finally, as a natural lull occurred, he called a halt.

Placing his hand over Francesca's heart he positioned an energetic cap over her heart chakra and closed it down to prevent further travel.

'That's enough now. You've been through enough,' he said. 'I'm going to close you down and give you some healing. Just relax.'

Francesca nodded and Mark channelled healing energy and light into her stressed body. She visibly relaxed and the lines dropped off her face, which took on a more serene look.

When he had finished she sat up and Mark passed her a glass of water.

'How are you feeling?' he asked carefully.

'Better, thanks. Much better. But exhausted.'

'I'm not surprised. That was a lot to go through,' he replied earnestly. 'It was enough for today, though.'

She hesitated momentarily.

'I think I can still feel something inside me. But that big one, which has been bothering me for years, has gone.'

'I know. That was a good job today, to get rid of that. We did well. Give yourself some rest today and take it easy. Allow yourself to settle down. I think you should see me again in a week's time to see how you are.'

'I agree,' she said fervently. 'I can't believe it is actually gone. That's amazing.'

'I know. It's great news I could help. Let's book you in for next week,' he replied.

A date was set up for the following week and Francesca left, with Mark's parting advice to drink plenty of water and take it easy.

Mark sat down. He felt drained. Never before had he come across anything like that. That was almost full possession. The spirit talking through her had been speaking in a language that Francesca said she had no idea how to speak. And he believed her.

And without knowing where he was she had looked straight at him with her eyes closed, following him as he moved silently round her.

Then there was the new ability he had used with his cosmic soldier guide. Removing it from a distance and flinging the entity high into the sky, without breaking a sweat. He could feel the power had come from his guide, but almost instantly knew he would potentially learn to do this more and more himself. His cosmic guide was just a facilitator for now. A catalyst and a teacher to guide him to this new ability.

Mark contemplated the events for a few minutes, mulling them over and replaying the scenes in his mind. He knew there was more to come. This wasn't the end. He had felt that when he closed her down.

He wasn't wrong. It came that night.

Author's Note

I have heard many people, including therapists, state that you should always leave your chakras open. This is not strictly true - let me explain why.

You are made of energy. Pure energy. Chakras are energy centres. Doorways into your inner self, to your inner energy. This can and often does allow negative energy in through the open doorway.

Like all doorways, things can move in as well as out. It's a two-way street. Your chakras are no different. You wouldn't leave all the windows and doors of your house open when you went out, would you? You may have some lovely people walk in, but you could also have a criminal or undesired person enter and wreak havoc among your prized possessions. Or even cause harm to you or your loved ones. So you wouldn't do it.

The same applies with your chakras. Learning how to open and close them at will is the secret. In fact it is a base learning: the control of and the awareness of your own energy systems.

From this foundation learning you can grow. And all growth should be set on strong foundations.

CHAPTER 29

NATIVE AMERICAN ANGER ATTACK

Night time arrived, and found Mark sitting at home relaxing. Having enjoyed his evening meal, he was sitting on the sofa watching some of his favourite recorded shows on TV. As was his norm, his black cat, Simba, was curled up on a cushion on his lap sleeping and purring.

Deciding he wanted a drink he carefully lifted Simba off, placing him to the side, and was rewarded with one lazy eye opening and a grunt of mild disapproval. Murmuring he'd be back in a minute, he went into the kitchen, poured himself a glass of water and re-entered the lounge. And stopped. Dead.

Something was wrong. The energy had shifted. Heightening his awareness he extended his senses, feeling for the source, and a few seconds later he felt it. There was a foreign presence, large and hostile. Immediately he pulled down his defences and started to focus, standing in his power as he gathered it around and within him. Stepping further into the room, the feeling of hostile energy increased. He peered deeper inside with his spirit eyes, seeking the source.

Slowly Mark walked across the floor and the dark energy source began to appear in front of him, just in the entrance to his healing room. Pausing, he watched the black cloud-like form shift and weave, trying to establish some form of coherency, till gradually it solidified, materialising into a vertical black oblong shape. Sometimes these things take time to appear in their true form, and can be slow to manifest before showing themselves as they truly are.

The energy felt somehow familiar, and he understood why when a large hostile Native American form stepped out from the dark mass. It was a portal.

Mark stopped moving and took it all in. Not one but several forms then appeared, all Native Americans, and continued to appear until there was a whole group of them, filling the end of the room from wall to wall. They stood there menacingly and he sensed that behind them was a great anger, with many more Native American spirits standing behind that were not yet visible but still within the portal, waiting to come through. He could feel their eagerness to join the fray, lending their energetic support to the immediate front-running group. This was a full attack group in a blatant show of strength.

Standing in his power, Mark quickly assessed the situation and knew the danger was very real. They had come to his home in retaliation for his actions earlier in removing a main player within their ranks, the one that had been controlling the portal within Francesca and using it for its own ends. He had disrupted that, and now they wanted vengeance. So they had sent a large attack force to take back what they believed was theirs and reinstate the portal under their control, planning to whip him into submission and defeat at the same time. Their intention was more than clear. It was a bold and aggressive move.

But they had made a mistake and underestimated him. It never seemed to surprise Mark how often they did this. Maybe it was the arrogance of these dark entities. The nature of the beast, so to speak. It's not that he couldn't be hurt. Of course he could. But they so often seemed to forget who he was and what he could do. Or be aware of the powers that worked both alongside and behind him, supporting and giving him his authority and strength.

Still, it was not without risks, and Mark well knew it. But there was a slight ego aspect to Mark that he had never quite managed to curb. In fairness, he needed this to believe in himself and to give him the strength to fight the dark ones. And he was angry they had assaulted him in his own home. His fortress. They had bypassed his usual defences and protection detail that was always in place about his house and thought they could get away with it.

They were wrong. He let the scene unfold, quietly gathering his power, allowing his anger to build, then spoke in a commanding tone to the first Native American, who was clearly the leader. But everyone present could hear him.

'You are not wanted here. Get out now,' he commanded, his voice ringing with authority. With his arms out to the side and palms facing outwards, Mark began to glow energetically, absorbing more and more power and filling every particle of his being until he could hold no more.

Staring at him, they leant forward, ready to attack as one. Mark's arms swept up and a barrier of light streaked across the room, slamming into their unsuspecting ranks with a force that stopped them dead in their tracks. Pushing forward, he slowly forced them back as they struggled against the unseen barrier keeping them from their foe.

Silently, white light soldier spirits appeared unbidden in a line alongside and behind him, strengthening his barrier as he slammed it into them with terrific force a second time. Shock waves ripped through their ranks, pushing them back towards the portal, destabilising and breaking their momentum.

He could see the waiting mass of the Native American soul group behind as he pushed, knocking many of them back as well. His guides upped their intensity as he gave another massive surge of power, bowling them over and back through the portal. Several managed to escape the first onslaught and flew behind him to attack from the rear.

Spinning on his heel Mark took hold of one and flung it into the waiting portal while still pushing the barrier into the main group. His guides worked tirelessly with him, supporting and lending their strength to everything he did. Light blazed around him and steely determination glowed in his eyes as he reached into every corner of the room, grabbing individual Native Americans and flinging them back though the portal.

As the last straggler was thrown behind the barrier towards the beckoning darkness Mark stood for a moment, now fully in control.

'You will not come back again. If any of you do I will destroy you,' he said with venom.

Gathering himself he made a final push, and shoved the remaining group of entities back through the gateway, resolutely slamming it shut behind them.

Looking around he checked the room for any stragglers, then extended his energy, carefully probing the rest of the house. Nothing. They had all gone. Taking a moment to collect himself, he thanked his guides with genuine gratitude for their help and sat down. Reinforcing his protection around the house he summoned soldier guides to line the inside of each main room. Four went on top of the roof and others patrolled the outside. He then reinforced his shield of gold light over the house like a dome and also under the property so no area was left uncovered.

Satisfied, he thought for a moment. That was ballsy. A full orchestrated attack by the entities he had removed earlier. There was more to this, he knew, and it would likely be coming to him sooner rather than later.

But for now he was safe. It was their move.

CHAPTER 30

THE HOUSE

Mark rang Francesca the next day and told her what had occurred. She was surprised, but also not surprised. She knew in her heart that it was a bigger problem but didn't know an attack like that could happen.

'Well, it's never exactly happened like that to me before, either. But we dealt with it. I just wanted to check in with you.'

'Thanks. I really appreciate it. I do feel better and I got some answers, but I know there are more to get rid of still. But just removing that first big one was a huge step for me. It's been there for years, and no one else has ever been able to get rid of it.'

'Well, it's a good start. We should book you in soon. Let it settle down for a while then come and see me. In the meantime I think we should look at your house. We need to cover all bases and I think it particularly important we do that with you, under the circumstances.'

'That makes sense. When would you want to come round?'

'As soon as possible, I think.'

'Well, I'm free the early part of next week. On Monday and Tuesday I am home all day.'

After quickly checking his diary Mark replied,

'Next Monday is fine. Is ten o'clock OK?'

'Perfect,' she replied.

'Good. I'll see you then. It's only a couple of days away,' and disconnected the call.

The weekend passed. Mark had the job with Francesca in his mind for most of that time, and it was with some anticipation he found himself driving towards her house, wondering what to expect.

As he drove onto her local estate he felt the energy shift. It went from neutral to rather sick very swiftly. When he was still several roads from her house he started driving slowly and looked around. It was dark and grey, which of course you could put down to the weather conditions. But it wasn't just that. And he knew it.

Several roads along it still felt sick, and Mark realised it was the entire estate and not just the immediate vicinity. All of it was sick. The land itself, and everything.

But he also saw something else. A vision, if you like. He was shown an image of a lawful large white elemental being standing at the side of Francesca's house, waiting and observing.

'So,' he thought. 'They are aware and prepared. Good.'

On pulling up outside he saw that it was a standard semi-detached house of typical design from the 1950's era, with a small front garden and a garage set to the side. Looking up at the windows he saw they looked dark and lifeless.

Getting out of the car he walked up the short path to the front door and knocked. A rucksack was slung over his shoulders with a few implements of his craft. They were minor things such as a sage bundle, matches, a copper Tibetan singing bowl and a crystal pendulum. They were not always used and on their own they wouldn't really remove anything. But they can help to clear the energy a little and provide a nice finishing touch if required after a clearing.

Francesca answered with a smile, and looked relatively relaxed. Stepping aside she gave him room to pass and he entered the house. Already fully prepared, with his defences in place and on high alert, he was direct and businesslike when he spoke to her.

He had heard from others that he looked totally different when entering a house he had to work on, even to the point of being a different person, and quite scary. One client, a therapist herself, took great pleasure in her introductions of him to others. How she had met him, and the way he had looked and made her feel when he entered her house. She had greeted him and then hurriedly grabbed her coat and left, making her excuses saying she would leave him to his own devices to get on with the job. In reality she had felt scared by his manner, and had been frightened by seeing a detached, intense man radiating power she didn't understand, who appeared quite intimidating. This was just her interpretation, of course.

Mark understood how he could come across. But once he was in Francesca's house there was little time for pleasantries and he was in full work mode, preparing for battle. After all, that was why he was called to most houses and land. To remove dark forces and entities.

She went into the kitchen to get him a glass of water, and Mark stood in the centre of the lounge and looked around. It was an open-plan design and quite spacious. A large leather sofa was behind him, close to the front bay window. An unlit fireplace was off to one side.

The room backed into a large conservatory, which in turn

opened into the rear garden. Small spiritual objects like Buddhas and crystals were dotted around on walls and pieces of furniture. You could tell that Francesca had tried to keep the place positive and peaceful. That was just a thin veneer, though, and Mark could feel the negative atmosphere underneath.

'Here you go,' she said, passing him the glass of water.

'Thanks. Why don't you show me around?' he suggested.

She nodded and took him around the house from room to room, working from the ground floor up. Most of the rooms felt a little sick. Some more than others. The loft in particular. Then she took him back downstairs and into the conservatory, leading him through into the garden via the patio door. The garden was approximately eighty feet long and forty feet wide, but the open space was significantly encroached upon due to the large garage residing within the grounds. At the bottom of the garden was a small river, and looking across the other side there appeared to be what looked like the back end of an old industrial estate.

He glanced over towards the garage and immediately sensed something within. A dark entity, which would need to be dealt with first.

Without looking at Francesca but focusing on the garage he spoke to her.

'Francesca, you need to go now. Something is in the garage and I have to deal with it first before I do anything else.'

His tone left no room for manoeuvre, and she knew him well enough to do as asked. Turning around she walked straight back into the house.

The garage appeared old and in need of renovation. An asbestos roof lay on top of concrete slab walls and a large grimy window was on one side. Already gathering his power, his defences increasing and ready to fight if needed, Mark moved to the front of the garage and opened the side door. The wooden door swung open easily and he stepped through.

The garage had the usual old equipment scattered about that you would expect to find. Numerous boxes were piled up next to a wooden workbench with a few tools on it. It was gloomy, despite the long fluorescent tube casting its light from the low beams above. Cobwebs hung around the roof and windows. In fact in many places. Clearly the garage wasn't used much.

After his first glance he was drawn to the corner by the boxes. Like most predators, dark beings sought to hide or ambush. So often they were in corners, or hiding in cupboards, wardrobes, or behind boxes or doors. Or just simply trying to merge into the background like chameleons.

When he focused his spirit eyes the energy became darker, then quickly coalesced into a black form. A dark elemental. Now it was in full view Mark stood opposite and spoke to it.

'What are you doing here?'

The elemental made no reply. It was almost a rhetorical question. Often they just don't answer, or they lie outright. But it's still a question you generally have to ask, if possible. Especially if you know it's of importance. But this one wasn't going to play ball. Mark got a sense of it just being there, spreading sick energy, and that it was part of the whole problem within the grounds, and indeed the surrounding estate.

'It's time for you to leave.'

Mark raised his hands and light glowed from within him, shooting out to form a bubble of light that surrounded the dark elemental. A few seconds elapsed before recognition slowly dawned of its situation, and then it started to struggle against its containment. But its attempt was half hearted and it didn't really want to fight.

Two light elementals appeared alongside it while Mark held

it securely in place. With one on each arm restraining, all three vanished.

The energy immediately started to lift. This elemental had definitely been one of the cornerstones holding the dark energy in place within the surrounding area.

Mark looked to the side and noticed a light satyr standing there, observing. Briefly he wondered how long it had been there, but guessed it had only just appeared as he started the removal or had arrived immediately after.

So, he mused, light beings were definitely watching what was going on here. This wasn't just about Francesca and her house.

With silent acknowledgement he exited the garage and went into the garden. Standing in the middle of the lawn he became still, connecting with the land and absorbing the ambience.

As he looked up to the sky, far in the distance, a large white being appeared, hovering a short distance above the land. After a few moments he knew who it was, the knowledge just appearing within. It was the spirit of Surrey. He paused to acknowledge him and relayed the information he had acquired since being here, detailing all his findings in the area. Mark concluded that he was still working on the problem. Finishing his report he stood still, patiently waiting for a reply.

The spirit of Surrey paused, then conveyed his response. Mark had found beings of greater power like this always seemed to communicate in a slightly different way, at a higher level than we do. It was almost as if the information just entered your mind. But it felt different too.

Because the spirit of Surrey was responsible for such a large area, and was a little above the day-to-day running of things, he was aware of a problem but not the full extent of it. He seemed to ponder over what he had been told for a few seconds. Then, grateful for the update and the information he disappeared, promising to look into the matter.

Mark nodded and walked down to the bottom of the garden onto a narrow paved area. A short metal fence marked the garden border. On the other side was a small river. Bigger than a stream, but not quite a river either, it was something in between. To the left it was blocked by natural debris, which slowed its flow to an almost imperceptible trickle, and the banks were overgrown and falling in. To the right, the end fence of the adjoining garden was a ramshackle wooden affair that barely stood upright.

The water was barely moving, almost stationary in fact and growing stagnant. Glancing across to the opposite side of the river he saw there was a high metal fence with various industrial-style buildings and warehouses, all looking in a state of disrepair. They were clearly unused and, equally clearly, had been so for a while. A couple of abandoned cars were to the right and vegetation had overgrown the whole area.

Mark's attention was drawn to some old wooden pallets not far from the two abandoned cars just the other side of the fence. There, watching him, was a large dark elemental. Roughly seven feet tall, he guessed, with a hard, dark body, it remained stationary as it observed him. Clearly it was the dominant elemental in charge of the local grounds.

If he was going to restore balance and shift the energy, this one had to leave too.

Standing opposite and slightly to the right, Mark called out in spirit speech,

'It's time for you to leave.'

'No,' it replied bluntly.

'It's time to leave,' Mark repeated. 'Your time here is done.

You will be reassigned. But it is time for you to leave. And you will leave,' he finished, with a note of finality.

'No,' it repeated.

Mark knew there was no alternative, and negotiation was pointless. This was just a local, more powerful dark elemental that was part of a bigger picture, and which had moved in to control the area.

Several seconds later a large white elemental appeared alongside Mark on the lawn. It was a lawful light being that clearly had been waiting for just this moment. More evidence that the powers that be knew what was going on, and were waiting for him to facilitate the transition.

Because it was bigger than its dark counterpart this changed the balance of power, and the dark one across the river knew it. It didn't particularly want to fight, and seconds later the light elemental appeared next to the dark one and picked it up and took it away.

A light satyr appeared where they had just been and stepped forward a little. This would be the being in charge of the area now, and would re-establish lawful control. As mentioned before, satyrs were a common choice of elemental in charge of land. Known to be fair, intelligent, and possessing natural management abilities, they were the perfect choice. A non-verbal request was made to Mark, which simply entered his mind.

'Do you want more?' he replied.

Silent confirmation again entered his mind.

With just a thought, he summoned half a dozen smaller light elementals, who appeared opposite alongside the satyr.

There was a pause, and a knowing entered his consciousness.

'More?' Mark asked with a questioning tone, raising his eyebrows.

With another thought a full dozen light elementals appeared opposite, alongside the others.

Mark looked over, silently questioning, and knew it would be sufficient. There was enough to get the job done and all the help it needed for now. They would clear the industrial estate and the river of sick energy, restoring health and vitality to the surrounding land.

It would take time, but it was a start. Changing sick land to a positive and healthy state always took time. Sometimes years. It could be a slow process. But, eventually, life would come back, along with vitality. Then everything that lived on that area of land would start to feel better. Plants would grow. Animals would return. People within their homes would feel better, and it would become a happier, more peaceful and prosperous environment.

Turning round he walked across the lawn towards the house, and stopped half way. He stood as a beacon of power and light with lawful authority. There was a dark feeling here also and he waited, probing.

Smaller dark elementals of various sizes popped into visual existence and Mark looked about. He called out to them and more appeared. They meant no harm to him. He knew they were just following orders, and were there at the bidding of the larger commanding ones.

With a wave of his hand he created a dark portal just a few metres away, and called them over. They obediently came towards him and, with a promise of relocation and assignment on the other side, they all trooped through and vanished.

Moments later, at some unsaid signal, light beings appeared in the garden to take control and facilitate a further transition.

Mark took a few seconds to feel the energy. Satisfied the outside was sorted, he walked back into the house and started to walk around downstairs, tuning in to see where where he was needed next. Then he heard a menacing voice from somewhere within, pitched in that unmistakable dark energy arrogance.

'You won't get rid of us,' it hissed.

Author's Note

When working in such fields as this many different spirit beings are used, depending on the circumstances and what is needed. While the physical person in charge will often ask for certain spirit beings to help, often the right ones just come, and can swap over numerous times during a job for whatever is needed in that moment. An example of this is jumping from spirit guide to soldier guide seconds later. Of course, the greater the ability of the person doing the work, the greater his authority, and the greater the number of tools and beings he will have access to.

Chapter 31

Underworld Cavern

The open-plan living space downstairs, while not feeling good, had little of specific interest. He walked over to the staircase and looked up. It didn't feel good. Cream carpets covered the stairs and rendered his steps almost soundless as he ascended. The further he went up the worse the energy became.

Stepping onto the long landing he paused. Approximately fifteen feet in length and several feet wide, there were six doors leading off it, three on either side. Carefully moving forward, with his senses on high alert, he walked past the first two doors and looked inside the next one along.

It opened into a medium-sized bathroom with a white shower cubicle, separate bath and toilet. Despite feeling sick it was free of any negative energy forms. The second door he opened turned out to be just a cupboard containing the hot water tank and boiler with no space other than for a few clothes to dry. Although small spaces can often house dark entities or energies, this was devoid of anything untoward. The next door opened into a small third bedroom with just a single bed inside and was free of clutter. While also feeling sick, this too was clear.

Drawn to another door across the way, he turned his attention to it and entered. Standing next to a large double bed in the centre of the bedroom was a large black demon. About six feet tall, it looked at him with black, lifeless eyes. Embracing his power, Mark moved across the room and stood a few feet away from it. His hands glowed as streams of light extended across the space between them. Held tight, the demon could not move.

After pushing it back into waiting hands Mark's spirit guides took it away.

A second demon of equal size appeared immediately alongside where the first one had been and Mark's hands shot out. Light beams secured it where it stood. Two spirit guides appeared, one on either side of it, and took hold of one arm each.

'What are you doing here?' he asked out loud.

The demon made no reply.

'What are you doing here?' he repeated more firmly.

It hesitated, and a whisper entered his mind.

'Contract.'

Mark understood what that was. He also understood that this demon didn't know much else. It didn't have the authority.

Pushing it away he nodded to the spirit guides, who promptly vanished taking the demon with them.

Scanning the room he saw an old wooden wardrobe and opened the doors. Inside he found three small low-level demons and yanked them out, passing them to waiting spirit hands, who took them away also.

Standing back he beamed white light into the wardrobe, clearing away dark energy and neutralising any negative residue. Quickly he brought down light into the whole room as a first-level shift of the energy and cleansing.

Exiting the bedroom Mark crossed the hallway to the last door and entered the main bedroom. Bigger than the previous one, it had an enormous queen-size bed in the centre. Built-in wardrobes extended along one wall and a dressing table sat underneath a large bay window looking out on to the garden. The energy didn't feel so bad in here and Mark knew this was where Francesca slept, which surprised him, as she had told him she slept badly and suffered nightmares.

Often Native American spirits tried to gain control of her and pierce her natural defences while she was asleep or at rest. The attacks were much more powerful at night than during the day, which was understandable, as your defences can be lower at night, when you let go of everything.

This can be countered with knowledge and awareness and by improving your connection to the energetic and spirit realms, so you obtain higher-level protection from the light spirits. You can also develop and enhance your own energy systems, learning control and awareness so your protective measures stay intact. Asleep or not.

As he honed his senses Mark caught wind of something behind him and spun around in a flash. His shields slammed down and his power escalated instantly. Raising his hands a barrier of white light shot out in front of him, just stopping the lunge of a large black demon. It struck the shield and howled in anguish at the loss of its victim. Mark lashed out and slammed into it with light, forcing it back against the wall. A full head taller than him, its inky black eyes glowed in malice as two lawful dark elementals appeared, one on either side and restrained it.

Looking directly into its eyes, Mark spoke out loud.

'What are you doing here?'

It made no reply.

'What are you doing here?' he repeated more forcefully.

The demon looked at him with undisguised malice and remained silent. As he studied it carefully Mark reasoned that apart from its obvious desire to not answer, equally it didn't know that much. He received an unintentional whisper in his mind of the word 'contract' again.

Realising he was unlikely to get any more information, he gestured for the two lawful dark beings, that he had summoned with barely a thought, to take it away. A dark portal opened behind them and they vanished inside, the portal closing behind them.

Walking out he entered the fifth and final room. Although it felt sick, it had no dark beings either. Taking a deep breath he walked back downstairs into the main living area. Francesca was there, sitting in the lounge waiting for him to finish. Briefly he outlined what had occurred.

She was not surprised and allowed him a moment to gather himself, as he sat down and sipped some water. Some minutes later, feeling rested, he continued.

'The main problem here is upstairs and in the garden. I've dealt with the garden and cleared upstairs, but I need to double-check. They don't seem to know much, except they're all talking about contracts. Meaning they have been given a contract from someone or something to be here and cause a problem for you in the house.

'I think this is all connected to your previous life. But I also think there is a bigger picture going on here. For a start, the whole estate feels sick to me. So it's not just you. But you are a focal point here, for sure.'

Francesca made no reply. Mark seemed deep in thought again as his eyes lost focus and looked off into space. In reality, what he was actually doing was letting go of his physical senses and allowing his non-physical senses to take precedence, which was vital when he was working.

Closing his eyes he scanned the house, searching.

Moments later he opened them and looked back at Francesca.

'There's something upstairs still. I'm not sure what, though. I'm going upstairs to check it out. You have a loft, yes?'

'Yes,' she replied.

'How do you get in? Does it have a drop-down ladder or something?'

'Yes, it does. There's a rod to open the loft hatch and pull the ladder down. I'll show you.'

She got up and led him upstairs, then opened the boiler cupboard and pulled out two rods. One was for opening the loft door and the other for pulling the ladder down.

'OK, you can leave it with me now. Thanks,' he said.

Reaching up he opened the loft door, which swung down, showing the metal ladder, which he hooked down onto the floor. He climbed up a few steps till his head rose just above the opening, where he saw a light switch just to the side and flicked it on. A bulb sparked into life and he pushed his head fully through.

As he looked around he saw it was quite a large loft, far longer than it was wide, almost rectangular in shape. The bulb did not pierce the darkness that effectively but he climbed up and stood on the rafters, peering into the gloom at the end as best he could.

For a full minute or two he looked, feeling. But saw nothing and made his way back across the rafters to manoeuvre himself safely onto the ladder, then climbed down till his feet hit the floor.

Wondering if he had got it wrong, he stepped away. And stopped. There it was again. That sense of something there. Turning around he climbed back up the ladder and re-entered the loft.

Refusing to be deterred this time, and determined to get answers, he flicked the light back on and looked harder down towards the end of the loft, right in the corner where it was darkest.

Tuning out his physical eyes slightly, he concentrated on his spirit ones and an indistinct shape began to coalesce. Having located the potential threat, he could now focus on it. The entity was going to great lengths to remain hidden. His eyes squinted as he stared intently, and the shape started to take form.

Roughly circular and two or three feet in diameter, it remained in the corner, showing no sign of having seen him. Its mass seemed to pulsate and ripple, and writhing tentacles extended from it, swaying from side to side, as it glowed a mix of dark sickly green over black.

Mark studied it. It appeared to be something like the brain or nerve centre of the goings-on within the house, but it didn't think independently. He hadn't seen anything like it before. But it was dangerous and emanating dark hostile energy.

Needing no invitation, Mark shot out white light and took hold of it. The light formed a ball of energy which encased it, lifting it up in the air. Its tentacles reacted wildly and flailed around, protesting at confinement and being moved. Reinforcing its containment, he waited till it was secure and then his spirit guides came down and hauled it away. Immediately on disappearing, the whole energy of the house shifted and became lighter.

Mark poured light into the loft, penetrating all the darkest corners in particular, leaching away all the residual dark energy and any roots and cords left by the unwelcome intruder.

Climbing back down he returned the ladder and closed the loft hatch before walking downstairs.

Thinking it was finished, he sat down in the now empty lounge to tune into the house as a whole. But minutes later he felt something again.

Entering a deeper meditative state, he switched off his physical senses and slowly a vision started to form. A picture, if you like. As he heightened his non-physical senses the picture started to become clear. And then opened into something totally other-worldly.

A dark space below the house grew, getting larger and larger until the scene below opened into what appeared to be a huge cavern within the underworld. Depth appeared to have no real concept here within this physical reality, but it was enormous and somehow unlimited. Fire was disgorged from fissures occurring at irregular intervals and lava flowed through channels interspaced with pools of bubbling red-hot magma. Huge stalactites and stalagmites had formed in various places amongst the almost endless expanse of rock floors and ledges.

Standing within the cavern on a wide rock plateau was a large black demon lord. In full physical form it appeared to be at least ten feet tall, with eyes radiating red in glowing waves. Two large horns stuck out of its head and clawlike hands hung off its long muscular arms.

Never had Mark seen such a clear vision of an underworld cavern. Rationalising that this was clearly the source of the house and land problems, he wondered how he was going to deal with it.

The demon roared and stamped its feet. Momentarily puzzled about what to do, Mark watched as an answering roar came from a short distance away. Hidden from the scene below him, he sat transfixed.

Reacting to the challenge, another demon lord stomped into view. Several times the size of the first, it strode towards the smaller demon. Its hard black exoskeleton was its most striking feature, with bright red eyes burning out of its skull and two huge horns curved up from the side of it head. Its gaping maw was massive, and huge pointed teeth lined the inside. Moving ever closer the enormous demon lord roared a second time, the sound was deafening and the cavern fairly shook as it reverberated off the walls.

So much bigger was it that on reaching the smaller demon it simply raised its leg and stamped on it with one mighty taloned foot. A thunderous clap occurred on impact, with such force that the ledge itself shook. Mark watched in fascination as the smaller demon's physical form simply vanished in a cloud of black smoke.

The victorious demon lord stood to its full height, which seemed at least twenty-five to thirty feet high, and roared out its challenge. The sound was deafening, and it sent a shiver down Mark's back as it echoed around the cavern. As no answering call came the demon lord stomped off out of sight, with flames coming out of the side of its mouth.

Mark was stunned. What had he just witnessed? The first demon lord was clearly behind the trouble within the house and surrounding land. He paused and thought it through. The second demon lord must be working for the lawful authorities, and, at the bidding of a higher power within the dark realms, had taken action and removed the unauthorised problem of the first demon lord, which had clearly overstepped its boundaries … which meant that both the light and dark realms at some point in the higher levels were working together and had both acted, once he had initiated events. It was like a snowball effect. He had thrown the first snowball and the whole thing had run wild and just got bigger and bigger.

While he was still in a meditative state the scene below came to an end. He had a feeling he was still being trained and tested. This was no surprise to him, as he realised that he was always being trained and tested. But it was another thing altogether to have something like that put right in front of you.

After sitting for a while Mark gathered himself together and examined the house room by room. There was no trace left of any dark influences or entities. Satisfied, he called down light from above, flowing down from roof to ground level, missing nothing, cleansing and clearing any dark energy residue as it came.

He stood up and looked for Francesca, and found her busy in the kitchen. Deciding not to tell her about the cavern scene, he kept his account of what had happened brief, but told her enough to keep her informed to her satisfaction. She didn't need to be even more worried at the moment, her knowing everything served no purpose.

'Why is all this happening?' she asked.

'That's a good question. Give me a second. Let me see if I can find out.'

He closed his eyes and thought the questions, and as soon as he was able to receive them, the answers flashed in his mind as quick as thought. Opening his eyes again he looked at her and spoke.

'It seems that you made an agreement when you were in spirit. To do certain things, which revolved around you working for the greater good while correcting any past ill deeds and mistakes. You were keen to do this. But, once you were in the physical world, things changed. You forgot about the agreement and then were unable to deal with it all. Now you are overwhelmed with everything.' He paused and, looking at her, continued. But this time spirit talked through him directly.

It will all work out in the end. You will understand all in the end. Even if you have to wait till you finally cross back into spirit.

Spirit left him and Mark looked at Francesca. She was connected enough to realise that spirit had spoken through him. She looked pensive.

'Well,' she said with a tight smile. 'I feel a little better now, and at least have some understanding of what's going on.'

Mark returned her smile, with understanding and empathy in his expression.

'It will get better. We'll get to the bottom of this. This is a time for you to grow, and there is a bigger picture involved here. And you are not alone, you have help and support. I'm not going anywhere, Francesca.'

'I know. And I'm so grateful to you, Mark. Thank you.'

With that Mark left and Francesca sat back down. Both remained deep in their own thoughts.

Author's Note

Using lawful dark beings or lawful light beings for a specific task can vary. Sometimes the greater powers make the decision for you and the beings are simply sent. On other occasions you just know what to do and summon them without thinking. As always, it depends on the ability and the authority of the summoner in respect of what he or she has access to, and what would be granted by the powers that be.

Also, house-clearing or cleansing, removing entities and spirits, cannot be done by waving incense around or sage. This practice is commonly called smudging. Nor can it be done by using Tibetan bowls or crystal bowls or any similar item. What they do do is help clear negative energy, breaking it down and moving it along, or freeing up stuck energy from corners and behind televisions or furniture. Smudging is a useful practice and it helps keep the room and house lighter and feeling more positive, especially when done regularly.

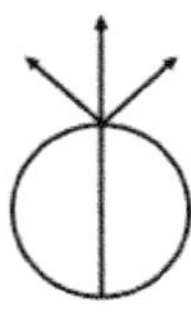

CHAPTER 32

INTRODUCTION

Francesca rang the next day and, recognising the number, Mark answered.

'Hi, Francesca, how are you?' he asked.

'Not bad, thanks. Still processing. Actually, I wanted you to see a very good friend of mine. We have worked together and spent a lot of time together over the last year or so, and he also has a problem. I am not sure how it's all connected, but he definitely needs you.'

'OK. What's his name?'

'Rajinder. He's an Asian guy, and I think he also has something dark within him. We've been on a spiritual course together and he told me about it. Do you mind if I give him your phone number?'

'No, not at all. Thanks. What about you? When do you want to come over again?' he asked.

'Is next Thursday OK? At 9:30 a.m.?'

'Sure, I'll book it in and see you then. If you have any major problems let me know.'

'OK. Thanks, Mark, I will,' and she hung up.

Later that day he received a text message on his phone from

someone enquiring about his services. He introduced himself as Rajinder, a friend of Francesca's. After a brief exchange Mark agreed to see him and an appointment was made for him to come over the next day.

Chapter 33

A New Input

The three beings of the secret order sat in their space within the clouds, observing and watching as always. Knowing their next course of action, Red Shaman spoke out loud without turning.

'If the members of the council wish to know more, let's get them involved in this one. It's time he received another test, one that Michael himself should administer.

'Let him report back to the elders. It's better if it comes from him. They'll listen to him and it should keep them satisfied for a while. Besides, Michael will be willing to do this. He likes to help, and this idea will appeal to him.'

He turned to his subordinates and looked at both.

'Make it happen,' he commanded.

The two subordinates, Malek and Abatheer, knew when their superior's mind was made up on a course of action. Without hesitation, they leapt into the air and flew at bewildering speed into the heavens above, eager to do his bidding.

Chapter 34

Uncles

The next morning Mark was up bright and early, in anticipation of Rajinder's visit. Having prepared his therapy room, cleansing, shielding, lighting his scented candles, and placing everything in its correct position in readiness, Mark meditated and waited patiently for his arrival.

Rajinder turned up punctually and Mark found himself facing a tall, slim man of over six feet with dark skin and black hair. Gentle of demeanour and immediately affable, Mark liked him. Yet there was a tightness to his bearing belying the problem underneath. Mark guessed that he was in his early to mid thirties.

He stood back to allow him in and closed the door behind him.

'Hi, Rajinder, how was your journey?'

'OK, thanks,' he replied with a smile.

'Good.'

Mark poured him a glass of filtered water, which he held while Rajinder took off his outer coat and shoes. Waving him through the doorway into his lounge and healing room he followed him through.

'Take a seat anywhere on the sofa, Rajinder. Move the cushions around as you see fit.'

'Thanks,' Rajinder replied, sitting down at the end of the sofa closest to the door.

Mark placed Rajinder's glass of water on the coffee table full of crystals in front of him.

'That's for you, by the way,' he said, indicating the water.

'Thanks.'

After sitting down on his chair at forty-five degrees from Rajinder, Mark watched and assessed his new client as he in turn swivelled slightly to look at him.

'How can I help?' he asked, leaning back, relaxed and focused.

Rajinder paused and his energy shifted, becoming more agitated.

'It all started a few years ago. I'm from Turkey originally but I've been in the UK for several decades now; a lot of my relatives live in Turkey still. I have a difficult relationship with two of my older relatives and they are, I believe, trying to control me.'

'How?' Mark asked, curiosity piqued.

'They are sending spirits and demons to attack me.'

Unfazed by this candid revelation, Mark spoke.

'How do you know this?'

'Because they want to control me. Since my father died my two uncles have taken control as head of the family and just want to know what I am doing all the time.'

'Do they practise this kind of thing? Dealing with bad spirits and demons to attack and manipulate people?'

'Yes' Rajnder replied. 'I know they do these kind of things.'

'Why don't you just walk away from them?'

'I have a house in Turkey which I need to sell, and I need to go through them to sell it.'

'I see. Why do you need them if it's your house? Can't you just sell it on your own?' Mark queried.

'Technically I guess I could. But everyone knows my uncles

and me there. It would be very bad form to just pass over them. It's not the way it's done, and they would probably try and block it as they are so well known in the area. They would force me to go through them.'

'I see,' Mark replied.

He sat back and thought for a moment, while tuning into the situation.

'I think we can do something about this. We need to deal with them. And whatever else is with you.'

While they were talking Mark had noticed a shadowy presence in the corner opposite at the other end of the sofa. This was a place where good and bad spirits seem to be funnelled in. He never really knew why it was that spot there. But generally that was the place, and he guessed it was just what his people and the universal powers had arranged.

Mark leant forward slightly, and his manner became more intense.

'Wait a moment,' he said to Rajinder. 'Something is here, and I may start speaking to them out loud. I may also travel out of my body and allow my spirit to deal with them spirit to spirit. So even though it may look like I'm doing nothing, I am.'

Rajinder nodded in response.

With that he leant back. Rajinder also sat back, and closed his eyes just before Mark did. Clearly he was connected, and aware too, at least enough to accept and act accordingly.

Mark focused, drawing a deep breath, feeling his feet on the ground and focusing his power within. Feeling his guides around him, he observed the shadowy energy. Two forms appeared, both of Asian appearance. Watching both forms, he spoke to them.

'What do you want?'

The answers just appeared in his mind, rather than him actually hearing the words. It's a much faster way of communicating than the physical spoken word and commonly used.

'We are here. We are entitled to be here.'

He sensed an arrogance, a belief that they had every right to be there. It came with a cultural understanding from their background that these prominent family elders were heads of the family and controlled things completely. Surreptitiously, if needed, and often going to any lengths to exert said control. Even to the point of employing dark arts to do so, which was and still is, a readily available and accepted practice among non-westernised societies. It was an old way of doing things and very common in people from this cultural background. It was the old guard, so to speak, still trying to hang on to the old outdated way of doing things. Times were changing and this was a dying, antiquated practice.

Mark guessed they would be arrogant, deceptive and stubborn, and was prepared for them being so.

'No, you're not,' he replied out loud. 'What do you want?'

Rather than a direct answer he could feel that sense of arrogance, and that they were manipulating and using dark energies to exert power and control over him.

Shrugging off their gathering dark energy, he spoke firmly.

'You need to stop and go away. You're not welcome here.'

They made no effort to move or stop what they were doing. Indeed, they carried on with an air of apparent impunity and belief in their absolute right to be there.

Immediately Mark shifted his energy and stepped out of his body and stood in front of the two dark beings in his own spirit form, glowing bright white in contrast to the two dark energies. His spirit guards stood behind him in a very visual show of strength.

The two dark forms failed to mask their surprise at his sudden appearance in his own energy form.

'You will go,' he said forcefully in spirit speech. He was physically silent to the outside world, but very audible within the spirit realms.

They stood still and watched him, surprise still masking their faces. Their arrogance had not let them consider that he would be able to do this. Indeed, their arrogance had led them to believe they could not be touched. They were wrong.

Mark erected a white barrier that pushed them back into the wall with ease and pinned them down. They looked back at him with a mix of outrage at his impudence and fear at this unexpected show of strength.

'Now you *will* go. I have told you to go and still you have not gone. Are you really stupid enough to believe that you can stand here in my stronghold and do as you wish? Universal law prohibits you from attacking him. He is with me. You have been told.'

With a negligent push Mark sent them flying back some twenty metres, where they were immediately held by the spirit guards waiting there. With a flick of his hands he flung them back to their bodies in Turkey, where they landed with a jolt. Too shocked to make any attempt to return, they just sat there dazed and bewildered.

Leaving them to mull over the result of their actions, Mark re-entered his physical body, pausing for a few moments to reorientate himself. It was always thus after projecting his spirit and travelling outside his physical body. For some reason it fatigues the body to do this.

He opened his eyes and looked at Rajinder.

'You can open your eyes now. It's done.'

Rajinder did so and Mark explained the situation.

'It was your uncles, yes. They are trying to control you. I

pushed them away, so we'll see what happens.' He paused. 'They were quite surprised, actually, though shocked would be a more accurate description. Angry at first, and arrogant, but not now. This will give them something to think about now, for sure.'

'Thank you, Mark. I could feel them go away. It was amazing,' Rajinder said, with gratitude.

'No problem. You have power, Rajinder, I can see that. But you've been held back by them. They don't want you to grow. They are jealous of you and your light, and angry that you have left their control and are refusing to be drawn under their influence again,' Mark said seriously.

'You need training, to help you gain strength and step into your power. You can learn to block them and close yourself down. And you can enhance your own power. I can teach you.

'Let's start with a basic meditation that I use myself all the time. It will teach you to ground, draw energy up from the earth, open your chakras, heal them, close them, shield yourself, call your guides in and heighten your awareness of energy, within, and outside eventually. I call it my foundation meditation.'

'That sounds great,' Rajinder replied enthusiastically.

Chapter 35

The Sword

Mark sat back and was about to close his eyes when he noticed a small dark form behind Rajinder, just over his left shoulder. Stopping what he was doing he looked carefully. It seemed non-hostile, but Mark needed to know what it was doing here.

'There's something behind you,' he said to Rajinder. 'I'm not sure what it is at the moment but I need to deal with it first.'

Mark turned his full attention to it. Relatively small, roughly circular in shape, almost like a blob, it still appeared to be non-hostile.

'What are you doing here?' he asked in spirit speech, thinking it may just be hanging around and seeing what was going on.

It gave an impish smile, if one could call it that, with what appeared to be a sense of mischievous humour.

Mark paused for a moment and knew it was best to just remove it.

'Right, then,' he said. 'You need to go. Time to move.'

He reached out with light cords to remove it and send it away. It squirmed with an apparent light sense of humour while at the same time the cords seemed to just slide off, leaving the spirit firmly planted on his shoulder still, unaffected by what he had tried to do.

Mark pushed a little harder, but again the spirit squirmed out of the way, somehow allowing his cords to just slide off as before. For some reason Mark was unable to grasp its form. Still it showed no outward sign of hostility.

Mildly perplexed, Mark frowned slightly and upped the power again significantly. This time his cords took hold and didn't slide off. The spirit reacted and started struggling to get free, attempting to shake off the restricting cords. And still Mark found it difficult to hold it securely.

Something didn't feel right, and a little doubt crept into his mind about what he was really dealing with. Deciding enough was enough, he spoke firmly.

'OK, that's enough now. You need to move.'

As he started to tighten his grip to force it to move, there was a moment's shift within its energy. Mark barely had time to register this, as without warning in front of his eyes the entity morphed. Growing in size and turning darker, its energy suddenly shifted from mild and almost childlike to outright aggression. Its power, until now hidden, ramped up proportionally. Multiple tentacle-like arms sprang out of its side and flayed wildly, lashing out with dark energy. Instantly he knew each one could cause significant harm if they connected with him.

Mark stood up, his shields slamming into place. Stepping into his power, he reinforced his restricting bonds and gathered his strength.

The entity grew again, and was now almost double the size of what it had been. And it went wild. Long tentacled arms stretched out in all directions, reaching out for everything and anything. Its power grew exponentially, shedding any similarity to its previous appearance, which had clearly been a ruse to be left *in situ.*

Slippery and still hard to hold Mark sent yet more power into his bonds. But it was like trying to keep hold of a greased wild pig going berserk. The struggle continued as he tried to maintain his grip and move it towards a waiting gateway that had appeared to the side, dodging flailing lethal tentacles in the process.

Bolts of power shot out from his hands in a desperate attempt to gain control. But it wasn't enough. And he knew it. This was a vicious underworld creature, and if it escaped he and Rajinder would both be in real trouble. He couldn't allow this monstrosity to roam free and cause mayhem in the physical realm.

As the seconds went by the entity continued to grow in intensity and ferocity, seeming to gain more power with each passing second. The situation became dire and Mark was moments away from losing his grip. Desperately he called out for Archangel Michael's help.

Michael appeared instantly, stepping straight into Mark's body and using him as a vessel. The light bonds that struggled to hold the entity in place solidified. Seeming not to come from his own hands any more, the power ramped up and intensified significantly, holding it fast.

The hybrid of Mark and Archangel Michael strode determinedly forward two paces towards the now berserk dark entity.

Mark dispassionately observed as a huge glowing sword appeared in his right hand out of thin air. Grasping it with both hands, he lifted it high above his right shoulder. His muscles bunched and with one fluid motion the sword arced down, cutting clean through the dark one's body.

The entity hung motionless in mid-air for a moment, as though in shock. Then, with a shudder, the body slowly slid apart, the tentacles trembling in their death throes. Not waiting to see the result, Mark/Michael hybrid reached over, and with a mighty backswing cut the demon in half again horizontally, his blade exiting in a silent energetic spray as bits of the dark one flew off in all directions.

Standing back, sword ready to sweep again and deliver its deadly message, he watched it sink downwards in four separating pieces, slowly dissipating into nothing as it died. Lowering his sword, the hybrid of Mark and Archangel Michael stepped back and Michael stepped out of Mark's body, separating them once more into two individual beings.

Stunned by the sudden, controlled ferocity and finality of Michael's actions, Mark looked at him. While he had only been the vessel, he could nevertheless feel the emotion and sensation of Michael's actions.

His unspoken question was answered.

'It was necessary. That thing could not be allowed to live. It had crossed over into our realm and had to be dealt with. It was far too dangerous, and there was no other way. You can't reason with that creature.'

'What was it?' he asked.

'It has no name as such that can be understood in your tongue. But it was a creature from hell that could not be allowed to stay free and was too dangerous to send back. It was the only way.' Mark understood. And with a nod, Michael vanished.

Opening his eyes he looked at Rajinder, whose own eyes opened seconds later and returned his gaze.

'I felt that. Something was very heavy behind me. Nasty. Now I feel lighter,' he said.

'Yes,' Mark replied. 'It was very nasty, a creature from the underworld. I had to call in help to deal with it and Archangel Michael came. It was very hard to remove and send back, but it couldn't be allowed to get free and roam our plane of existence. It would have caused a lot of problems, traversing the globe and generating chaos wherever it went.' Mark paused. 'Actually, that's an understatement.'

Rajinder looked at him wide-eyed. Respect showing clearly on his face.

'That's amazing, Mark. I could actually feel some of what you were doing … but why was it with me?'

'That is a good question. Why indeed? This may be part of a bigger picture. I'll have to tune in and ask. Give me a moment.'

Mark tuned in and emptied his mind, letting go of his physical self and allowing spirit to come through. He asked the question in his mind,

'What is happening here?'

Spirit answered and Mark repeated it out loud.

'It seems you were connected in a previous life to Francesca. And part of the same soul group at one time. You are no longer part of that soul group. But still the connection is there. Yet that is not the only reason.'

Mark paused. Not wishing to tell Rajinder the whole story, he considered his words.

'Also there is a bigger picture going on here, Rajinder. I have noticed that a lot more of these darker cases are coming out. More people are being attacked by dark entities. There is a shift in the energies, and a global shift at that. With more people becoming aware and being affected, these incidents and experiences are being brought to my attention.'

Rajinder continued to look at him in amazement. Mark continued.

'But it should be gone now. You may have a few more problems with your two uncles, but we will deal with them. This is also part of your learning. I will teach you and guide you and give you support. But this is part of your learning and personal growth as well. I could easily have dealt with those two. It's well within my capabilities and I have done that sort of thing many times before. But I am being held back. It's because you are meant to learn from it, to grow.

'I'm seeing a lot more of these cases now where I am being allowed to only go so far, not remove them completely like I would have previously, but just deal with them up to a certain point, which allows the person affected to grow and develop. Also, the antagonists are learning from this, even though they don't know it. So there is a whole bigger picture of people growing and becoming aware.'

Rajinder listened intently as Mark paused for moment.

'It's just amazing, Mark, that this is happening, isn't it?' he said smiling.

Mark could see that Rajinder was not cowed by his revelations, but, rather, was excited and amazed. After logging that information he made a decision to begin teaching him some rudimentary topics within this field and see what would happen. He wasn't the first potential candidate in the last year or so and maybe he could be put to use later.

The rest of the session went by without mishap, with healing, meditation, and some basic tools for Rajinder to take home to help him.

Mark stood up, indicating the session was at an end, and showed Rajinder to the front door. He shook his hand and opened it for him, with a parting agreement that they would speak soon to arrange another session.

Mark sat back down in his lounge and reflected. An increasing problem was being brought to his attention. More and more dark experiences and attacks were occurring. Family attacks were on the rise as well. But this time there was a definite connection between Francesca, Rajinder and himself. Nothing happened by accident.

He could deal with Rajinder as and when, and put him to

one side for now. But Francesca was a bigger part of the picture. Somehow it just felt that way. The situation was escalating and the Francesca scenario had only just started, but it would lead to answers. And he was included in this picture somehow.

After mulling it over for a while he laid his mind to rest. The answers would come. He'd just have to wait. He'd heard from Francesca earlier and was due to see her the next morning, so he would need his strength. With that in mind he rested for the remainder of the day in preparation for the morrow.

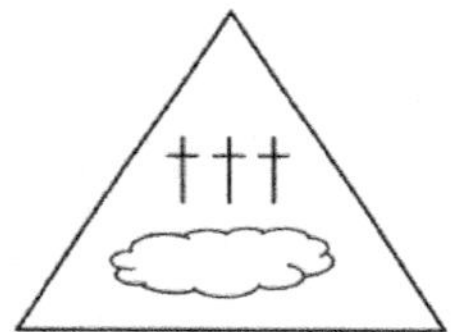

Chapter 36

The Clouds

Three beings sat in their lofty tower, as was their wont, overlooking the scene below. Realising at the same time they were no longer fully in control of events, but merely wheels in a bigger machine. Their influence had been reduced. But still they could, in some small measure, help. And Red Shaman wanted to help as much as he could. He had invested much in this human warrior of the Earth realms and did not wish to lose all that vested potential.

Michael had done his job, as Red Shaman had known he would. He also understood the bigger picture. Although he was not as immersed in the politics of the situation as the others he had willingly completed his part in Mark's training. The council of elders had received his report with only moderate acknowledgement. But, unable to find anything directly contravening their authority, they could say nothing and allowed the training to continue.

Waiting for their commander's next orders, Abatheer and Malek watched him carefully as a hint of an inward smile played over his features.

Now it was time to up the game. He looked across at his underlings and explained the next phase. They exchanged glances and Malek said what was in both their minds.

'That's a big move. Very big. Is he ready for this next wave?'

'It is a big move,' Red Shaman replied, 'but we have little choice. Events are moving faster than I thought and we must push him. Open the gateways to the other realm. Let's see how he deals with this.'

The two lieutenants turned away and whispered words of power in a language long forgotten to most. A portal opened far in the distance and they streaked off with an inhuman scream to enter a realm not of this world.

Author's Note

You will have heard it said, particularly by healers, that when doing light work you should not channel your own energy, but the energy of spirits or universal energy instead. One of the reasons behind this is so you don't get tired. Another is that the energy you channel is purer and more powerful.

While in a way this is true, the fact is that it all depends on what you are specifically doing, and how you work, and with which particular energies and/or beings you work with. It also depends on how advanced you are, and I don't mean in human qualifications. I mean in spirit qualifications, in what the powers that be have assigned to you, so to speak.

Some tasks are also much harder than others and can be extremely exhausting. For example, channelling powerful beings for messages or healing. Or using powerful energies and beings for land clearing, attachments, haunted property or battles.

The harder and more difficult the job, the more powerful the beings you use and work with and the more exhausting it is, just as it would be in the physical world.

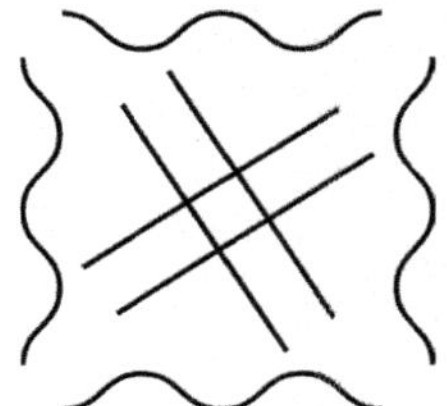

Chapter 37

The Takeover

The next morning came and Mark had done his best to prepare. The whole morning had been set aside for Francesca. He knew it was likely to be a difficult few hours, and because of this was slightly apprehensive about what might happen next. In reality he didn't know what would happen, and waited stoically for her arrival.

The doorbell rang and he opened it for her. Francesca entered looking tired, as though she had been having a difficult time again. Ushering her through to the lounge she sat on the sofa and he waited patiently in his chair opposite till she settled down. Judging the time to be right, he spoke.

'Well, Francesca, tell me what's been going on.'

She paused and reached for her notebook, opened it at the correct page, then glanced at her notes.

'I keep records of what happens so I don't forget,' she replied. 'Well, it has improved a lot since I last saw you. You removed the big main one I had had for years, and I really felt it. So thank you. But I still feel a presence within me and the urge to speak in Native American. So I think there is something still within me.'

'There is. I can feel it,' Mark replied. 'We'll deal with it.'

'Good. Also I feel that there is something else going on. Almost reptilian-like. I'm not sure. Maybe it was already there and I have only just noticed it because you removed the big one the other week. Or maybe it's just come. I don't know.'

'What do you mean, "reptilian"?' he asked carefully. Mark was very aware that people often bandy around the word 'reptilian' and other such names and clichés without really understanding what they are talking about.

'It's difficult to work out exactly. But they feel like reptiles. Crocodile-like beings. I can almost see them, and that's what they feel like. I get a sense that they are behind me and dragging on my arms. Particularly my left arm. It feels like a reptile. Giving me pain, and pulling at me. Actually on my leg too.'

Mark paused and looked at Francesca. He would not take what she said lightly, but had had no actual dealings with what he considered to be genuine reptilians in energy form.

'What do you think?' he asked.

'It's difficult to know what to think, as I don't trust myself any longer,' she replied earnestly. 'I feel as if Francesca has been taken over for so long now, literally years. I don't even know if I am myself, the true Francesca, or something different.'

Mark listened intently to what she said and watched her energies.

'I understand,' he replied, not unsympathetically. 'That will improve with time as you get answers and we clear what is going on with you. Let's see what happens. We'll do some healing first and look at the Native American issue first, then see what comes up with the reptilians.'

Leading her into the healing room she sat down in the high-backed brown leather chair and closed her eyes.

Mark looked at Francesca and tuned into her energies while moving behind her and placing his hands on either side of her head.

Channelling energy Mark's link with her deepened, enhancing his connection and therefore his access to knowing and information, all of which enabled him to heal on a deeper level.

As he started to move his hands around her body, clearing away various blockages, pulling them out and throwing them away, he was drawn to the heart centre and observed the portal within.

Placing his hands over the heart centre Francesca started to twitch and looked uncomfortable.

'What's happening, Francesca?' he asked.

'I'm getting pain in my chest and I can feel a presence in me wanting to take control. It's trying to talk through me but I am blocking it,' she replied.

'OK, give me a moment.'

Mark tuned in and looked deep into the heart centre where the portal was residing and a dark shape within stepped forward. Angry and aggressive, it sent waves of hostility at him.

Reaching into the portal Mark took hold of the spirit and tried to pull it out. But it was being supported by others behind, who now made their presence felt.

With his hands in place Mark studied the spirit and realised it was a Native American again. But this one was different. This one was from a rival faction to the previous being. And he had his tribe behind him. They had stepped in to take control of the portal and had seized the opportunity to step in where there was now an apparent power vacuum over the still-operating portal.

This gained them power in several ways, not least the control of the portal and the souls within. They chose those who crossed and who didn't to suit their own ends, demanding payment and sucking their life force when desired. This had put them in a very powerful position within the relevant spirit worlds.

Mark relayed the basics of this to Francesca as the information came to him.

'What do they want?' she asked.

'What do all these sorts of beings want? Ultimately, power,' he replied. 'Feeding off the souls. Control.'

'Why?'

'Why? You could ask that of all power-hungry beings, of human beings in the physical world as well. They just want it. And will do anything to get it and hold on to it. Don't worry. I'll deal with it.'

With that Mark braced himself and firmed his grip and control over the portal.

'Right, it's time for you to leave,' he said, speaking firmly to the main Native American within.

It wasn't a reply in words exactly, but it was very definitely not going to just leave. They wanted this and were not about to give it up without a fight.

Feeling power course through his body as he gathered himself, Mark gave a big surge as he reached in and grasped the main Native American, hauling him out of the portal. As Mark pulled him out, his tribe hung on trying to pull him back in. He could see the energy cords extending from him back into the portal. He'd never get rid of him while those cords existed. Like an elastic band, he would just be drawn straight back in.

Pulling him further out Mark walked behind Francesca holding the Native American at arm's length and passed him over to the hands of the waiting spirit guides, who held him fast.

Moving back in front of Francesca he ramped up the power travelling through him. His hand was glowing bright white, and with a large chopping motion he severed the cords, his hand cutting clean through as he watched them fall away. He reached in and pulled out the last of the negative hooks and attachments connecting the Native American spirit to Francesca, fully releasing it so it could be taken away.

'How do you feel? he asked Francesca.

'A little better. I felt him go. But I can feel there are more and they are angry. I can feel all their emotions.'

'I know. There is more to do.'

With the main one now gone Mark set about with vigour, reaching inside and pulling out other members of the tribe. It was like removing a rival gang from power in the 1920s, who had entered new territory and were controlling the roads and the area with fear and violence.

He pulled out one after the other of a seemingly never-ending line of wayward Native Americans and sent them away to be dealt with by spirit. Eventually, after what seemed to be the final one, he paused.

When he looked at Francesca he saw a tear run down her cheek.

'How are you, Francesca?'

'They've gone,' she replied. 'But I can feel so many Native American souls. They are so sad. The emotions are overwhelming.'

'OK. Try not to let them swamp you. You're Francesca, not all these other souls. Give me a moment and I'll release them.'

Mark shifted his energy to one of compassion and understanding. Reaching in he spoke to the waiting souls within. It was a two-way conversation that only he could hear.

'It's OK. You can come out now. Yes, you are free. You are released now and will be taken to where you should be. Your family are waiting for you there. Go with these angels and the light guides you can see just through the gateway ahead. That's it. Take my hand, walk along the path and go through the gateway.'

Mark released soul after soul through the beckoning light gateway, sometimes into the waiting hands of loved ones, others to friendly members of their tribe. Some went to kindly light spirit guides.

Tears ran down Francesca's cheek, interspersed with sporadic sobs as he worked. Every now and then she would raise her hand to dab away the tears with a tissue clutched in her hand.

Eventually, as the last one that had been waiting went through, Mark glanced at Francesca, and judged she had had enough. He too was tired and decided to call a halt to it.

'That will do for now,' he said. 'We've finished doing this, and you've worked hard enough.'

After trying to regain control for a few moments and allowing herself to settle down, she spoke.

'Why do they still keep coming through?'

'That's a good question. Let me see if I can find out.'

Mark stood still and closed his eyes in concentration, as he put out a silent request for someone in power within the Native American realms to come and answer his questions.

A large Native American being appeared in the room. It shone brightly, and Mark could immediately tell that it was one of power and was likely to be a low-level deity. If not, he was not far off.

Though decorum, and indeed his personal ethics, called for Mark to be respectful, he wanted answers, and he and Francesca deserved them. Someone had to be held accountable for the actions of these Native Americans. It was way too big to be ignored.

'What is going on here?' he asked the glowing form.

The being answered apologetically.

'We were aware of what was going on to a degree, but not the whole picture. They were a rogue element and are connected to an entire soul group. Francesca is or was part of this soul group and has much history with them. In a previous life she had power, and like all people of power, she upset a lot of other people. And so it got complicated.'

'That I understand, but she is not that person any longer and is on a different path.'

'We know. But she is still connected, and others have not

forgotten. She made an agreement, in spirit form, we believe, to make some amends. To act as a living portal to help Native American souls cross over. Unfortunately, other contingents got wind of this and sought to take control. Some to attack her, and others just for their own reasons.'

'This needs to stop,' Mark replied. 'She is Francesca now, and while she doesn't mind helping lost souls and those who need help to cross over it must be on her terms.'

The glowing form silently acknowledged this and spoke.

'I know. I will do what I can. We will act on this and try to put things in place. We will get control of this soul group and its wayward elements. Both within and out.'

Mark nodded in acceptance and the form disappeared.

He explained what had been said to Francesca as she listened intently, absorbing every word.

'So it should ease off now,' he concluded with a smile. 'Let's see if we can finish off. Just relax.'

Author's Note

Dark entities, when drawn from the body or aura, should always be taken away. Sent elsewhere. By whom depends on the circumstances. Or, if granted the power, they should be sent wherever is appropriate by the healer himself. This is rarer, but it can be done.

When removing simple negative energy and blockages, care should always be taken to ensure that the negative energy is appropriately disposed of rather than just flung out into the surrounding environment to float around and reattach itself to the client or someone else.

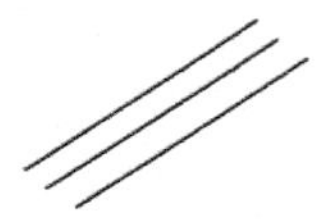

Chapter 38

The Reptilian Contingent

Positioning himself behind Francesca Mark refocused and tuned back into her energies again, placing his hands on either side of her head. After a few minutes he placed his hands on her shoulders, channelling energy through her body, and then transferred his attention to the still-present portal within her heart centre. Like a dark hole, it appeared to be empty. But it was still active. It was just that the flow of Native Americans had been stopped for now.

Focusing on the portal, directing energies to it, he sensed something else in there. Something new. Something different. As he looked in he saw what appeared to be a reptilian-like entity inside. Similar to a crocodile, but in a humanoid way, standing on two legs. It had intelligence. And others were behind it.

While observing this he became aware that something was on Francesca's back, which until now had remained hidden. Turning his attention to it he looked hard and a form began to take shape. A reptilian spirit was latched onto her spine. Focusing fully he didn't hesitate, and reached for the root of her spine and behind the neck of the creature. Taking a firm grasp he dragged the reptilian off, passing it over to the waiting soldier guides.

Stepping back from Francesca he cast a vigilant eye over her and saw several energetic reptile forms sitting within her aura. One by one he yanked them off and passed them across to the waiting guides.

Standing in front of her, he studied her energy fields. Satisfied she was clear for now, he focused his attention again on the portal and the reptilians within. They were angry. And aggressive. In fact, they were acting like you'd expect a crocodile to act. Aggressive, antagonistic and territorial. But with human-level intelligence and standing upright. And clearly not from this realm.

One of them moved forward aggressively, and Mark stepped further into his power.

'What do you want?' he asked, blocking its progress.

'This is ours,' it growled in a hissing voice.

He was talking about the portal. And Mark knew instantly they wanted control of it. He didn't know the exact reasons why. But one thing was for sure. They weren't good.

Reaching in Mark took hold of the reptile being and began to pull it out. Aggressively it clawed at his hands with crocodile-like appendages, and snapping teeth viciously reached for him.

With a surge Mark yanked hard and the reptilian was hauled out, snapping and snarling. He passed it over to the waiting soldier guides who took it away, its aggression undiminished.

Reptilian after reptilian was pulled out of the portal until Mark finally called a halt and took stock. Looking deeper with spirit eyes and a combination of all his spirit senses, he looked for an answer to where this endless stream was coming from. There was a depth to this as yet unseen.

Some long moments passed and something started to form, coalescing into what appeared to be a long black tunnel, a conduit, if you like, leading from Francesca's back out into the ether and seemingly endless. Quickly he sensed it was exactly that. A conduit to another realm. The reptilian realm. Wherever they came from they were using this conduit, this tunnel, to bridge the gap from their realm to ours. This had to be closed, and now.

Hairs suddenly stood up on the back of his neck. Turning his head around he saw that a large reptilian had appeared behind him. Spinning on his heel he raised his hands and a shield of light blocked the reptile's reaching claws, and his shield rapidly transformed into beams of attacking light. Pushing out his energy the light beams held it fast by the throat and lower chest.

Mark took a moment to observe it. Bigger than any he had seen so far, and one of higher rank than the others, it was clearly a direct response to his piercing the fog and seeing the conduit, which they had so carefully tried to hide.

Roaring its frustration, the reptile clawed ineffectually against Mark's bonds. Although it was contained Mark knew he had to get rid of it, and fast. The reptile was strong and straining desperately against its restraints to reach him. Any questions he had would have to be quick and to the point. Pushing an extra bolt of power into the reptile he spoke out loud in a powerful voice.

'What are you doing here?'

'This is ours,' it replied in its hissing voice. 'The gateway is ours. You will not prevent us from reaching your world.'

Mark tightened his grip.

'Really?' he replied in a deadly tone. 'I think not.'

Driving more energy through and with a mighty push he propelled the reptile high into the skies, where it hung helplessly like a small, squirming action figure. Almost immediately two light beings appeared either side of the reptile.

Mark looked closely. No, not light beings, exactly. Something different. Cosmic beings. Like policeman or soldiers, only on a cosmic level. They were a slightly different colour and feel to regular spirit workers. Something deeper, with an almost alien kind of depth and glow. Not quite white, not quite gold.

His examination of them was pulled up short as an instant later all three vanished.

Mark had little time to ponder over this new turn of events, as a new threat appeared and a demon materialised out of nowhere a few metres from him. Approximately six and a half feet tall, black, with a thick body, cloven feet and red eyes Mark knew instantly it was one of rank. Probably of lieutenant level.

Already standing in his power, Mark stood ready to counter whatever it was going to throw at him.

'What do you want?' he said out loud.

The demon just looked at him, making no move to attack, as though it was assessing the situation.

'Well?' he repeated.

In Mark's experience demons talk very little, and when they do it's a bare minimum. Only the very high levels or those of a certain type and role within the dark ranks offer much in conversation and answers. Even then, not a lot.

Clearly it was debating what to do and seemingly wondering how to deal with this unexpected turn of events.

Making his intentions clear, Mark could feel power both behind and with him. So could the demon.

Seizing his advantage, he repeated his question in a commanding tone.

'What do you want and why are you here?'

After coming to a decision it answered.

'Contract,' came into his mind.

Rather than words spoken out loud, these answers from spirit and other energetic beings almost always just enter his mind so he 'hears' and 'knows' answers within. With that new information came an understanding that somehow the underworld had been connected to the reptiles and this incursion into our realm. Or at least they were aware. Equally, the full extent of the situation was not known by this lieutenant.

'Whatever contract you had is terminated. Go back to where you came and don't return,' Mark said with absolute finality, leaving no room for negotiation.

A dark portal opened up in front of it and with only a moment's hesitation, the demon stepped in and disappeared.

Mark turned away to continue with Francesca. Then stopped. Turning around again he looked carefully where the demon had stood and stared at the spot for some seconds. Part of it was still there.

Employing an old and often-used trick by certain beings within the darker fraternities, it had allowed part of its energy to disappear, giving the illusion it had gone, while leaving its core still present and unobserved. Many people are fooled by this trick, even experienced soul rescuers and equivalent professions used to moving spirits on. But it didn't fool Mark.

Bolts of light shot out and held it fast.

Firmly Mark spoke directly to it, holding its gaze.

'You had your chance. Now you will be sent away and dealt with by the powers that be.' Catapulting it high up into the sky, two more cosmic soldiers appeared and took it away.

'Now you will be dealt with,' he called after it.

He returned his attention back to Francesca and focused, directing his energy towards her in a stabilising manner.

Speaking out loud, he asked for answers. Seconds later, as if in answer to his summons, another large reptilian appeared some feet away.

Mark took a step back. This was no ordinary reptile, and within seconds he realised this was very high-ranked within its own kind.

Cloaking himself in light and bracing to strike he looked at this new potential threat. The reptile stood there, making no overtly aggressive move towards him, and Mark took this brief respite in the confrontation to observe it. Its reptile form glowed. It was clearly some kind of high-ranked leader within its own realm. Standing about seven feet tall and totally reptilian in appearance, it stood on both hind legs and intelligence emanated from within.

'What do you want?' Mark asked again.

The reptile paused and then spoke.

'This is a rogue element within our world. It is not our doing.'

Suddenly Mark sensed a dark energy appear next to him. It was not hostile, but rather that of a lawful higher dark power. Instantaneously, and with no preamble, it slid into his physical body, gently but irresistibly pushing his conscious control to the side. Its power was almost overwhelming. And just like previously, when he had channelled such dark power, Mark struggled to keep himself present and grounded as the world almost spun out of control.

Seamlessly it spoke through him, and Mark became just a passenger within his own body. Within a moment he knew it was part of prime darkness itself. A representative. The ultimate dark authority, and light's opposite number within the universe.

'You are out of line,' said the representative of prime darkness in a deceptively quiet voice. 'Do you know who I am?'

Cowed, the reptile nodded.

'Yes.'

'You are upsetting the balance of things. You are not meant to cross into this realm. You are drawing attention to yourself within the dark realms and there will be consequences.'

The dark one looked intently at the reptile.

'I understand. We're sorry. We have been trying to resolve this but have failed. We will fix this.'

The dark one slightly raised its voice.

'Make sure that you do. The penalties for this incursion and flagrant breaking of the balance will have dire consequences for your realm. And you don't want that. Do you understand?'

While spoken quietly, the intensity and warning behind the words were very real and were not missed by the reptile leader.

Bowing its head, and with no small amount of desperation it answered.

'I know. We will do our best.'

The dark one held the cowed reptile's gaze for a few moments more, making sure it understood.

Satisfied it had heard and would be obeyed, Mark felt the dark one leave his body as quickly as it had come.

After a second's disorientation Mark swiftly gathered himself, gaining some semblance of self once more, and spoke to the reptile leader.

'You need to sort this out. And you need to do it now.'

'We will do what he can. We are trying to clean this up but have been unable to get hold of them all so far.'

It raised its clawed hands in recognition and made a gesture of a slight lack of belief that he would be able to fix this to the satisfaction of the dark one. And vanished.

Chapter 39

Portal Closure

Mark turned back to Francesca, who was still lying on the therapy couch. She was watching him, and he guessed she knew something big had been going on.

'There is a portal behind you. Or, to be more specific, a kind of conduit, a black tunnel through which the reptiles have been coming through. They have jumped on the bandwagon, so to speak, and seized an opportunity to hijack the control of your portal and use it to form a conduit into their realm. This is how they are getting through.'

Francesca looked surprised and perturbed, but not very much. Mark was impressed with the tenacity of this tall, connected woman who had been through so much and was still going through so much. She was strong, and needed to be.

'I have spoken to a large reptile being that appeared just now. It appears to be one in authority. It was aware of this group of reptiles but stated that they are a rogue element and they had been unable to pin them down and deal with them. So it appears that the powers within their own realm know about the situation.'

Mark looked at Francesca and quickly gauged what to tell her.

Deciding that a little prudence was best, he chose his next

statement carefully.

'Then a higher power came through and warned it about their transgressions. It said that they were upsetting the balance of things and to sort out this problem. They are drawing attention to themselves with the higher dark realms, and they really don't want to do that.'

Francesca's eyes were wide as she listened, and Mark continued.

'Now we have to close this conduit. That should end the incursion and also end using you as a portal to get across to our realm. OK?'

Francesca nodded and closed her eyes again. Focusing on the portal within her and the long endless black conduit stretching back behind, he focused his power. He could feel several light beings behind him adding their strength to his.

He raised his hands and directed energy through the portal and into the conduit itself, allowing the energy to build up. Unsure exactly how he was going to do this he relaxed and surrendered his conscious mind, trusting spirit to guide him and do what needed to be done.

With the intention of closing the conduit firmly in his thoughts the energy continued to build up, getting stronger and stronger. Mark could feel the power welling up within him, bolstered by the light beings behind. His whole energetic body swelled with the volume of energy he was pushing through the portal. As he looked deep inside, the conduit seemed to literally start folding in upon itself. He continued to watch as he poured in more and more light. The conduit gradually became narrower and narrower, shrinking in upon itself, until eventually it just ceased to exist.

Mark stood back a moment and observed the space where moments before the seemingly endless conduit had been. Satisfied it was closed completely, he returned his attention to Francesca's immediate aura and energy fields.

Focusing on her back, he then removed the dark residue where the conduit had been attached. Dissolving it in light, he watched the area become clear. Satisfied, he then cleared the last remaining energy and slammed the door shut on her back in finality. The last evidence it ever had existed disappeared completely.

Taking a step back he settled himself down and channelled pure white light into Francesca's body. A team of healing spirit guides circled her and pushed light in at the same time, cleansing and clearing her entire body and aura.

After a minute Mark went through her main chakras, checking and closing them down one by one, and finished by bringing down a white light shield around her, keeping her positive energy in and any negative energy out.

Looking around his healing room he brought down light throughout the room and every other room in the house, one room at a time. Then he placed a golden shield over the entire house, including everything underneath it so no part was left unshielded. Failing to do this thoroughly would potentially leave open access points into the premises, where dark forces could gain access. Quickly he summoned light soldier guards to form a ring outside the house, plus two on the roof and several inside each room.

Refocusing back on himself he grounded, pulling energy up and through his body to cleanse and empower himself, finishing with a white light shield around his body. Taking a step towards Francesca he gently touched her arm and spoke.

'Francesca. I'm finished now.'

'You closed the conduit?'

'Yes,' he replied. 'It's done.'

Letting out a breath she smiled.

'Good. Thank you so much, Mark. I can't thank you enough.'

'You're welcome,' he replied sincerely.

Helping her up from the couch she moved across the lounge and into the kitchen at the front of the house, gathering her belongings as she did so.

Mark looked her up and down in a last check before she left. Satisfied her energies were good, he spoke.

'Things should improve for you now. We've dealt with the hardcore stuff.'

'I know. I really can't thank you enough. No one else has been able to move the things you have got rid of. Especially that first big Native American. He's been there for years, and no one could get rid of him. And now the rest of it. Thank you,' she said earnestly.

'You are very welcome. I'll be honest … I don't think this is the end for you. This is all part of your journey of growing and evolving. As I said, we have dealt with the hardcore stuff. And having removed those things and the work we have done so far will enable you to move forward now. And I'll be right here for you. I'm not going anywhere. So you have my support, and I know we'll get Francesca back to her old self. With me teaching you and the continuation of the work by both of us, it will be better in the end.'

'Thank you. I'll be back soon. I want to learn and be clear of all this,' she replied.

Giving him a hug goodbye she opened the door and walked out.

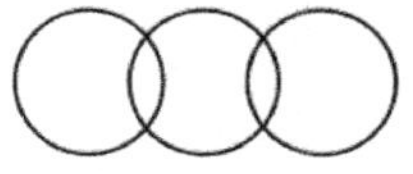

CHAPTER 40

SKY ATTACK

Mark watched Francesca walk down the path and closed the door behind her. He turned around and walked back into the lounge to start his cleansing ritual. Taking his rattle he moved around the lower floor, shaking it constantly and making sure he visited each corner in the process. This helps to dispel any negative and stagnant energy. Then, asking spirit to help, he called down light again through the entire house. He watched his light workers form a line and sweep through the house, clearing the energy as they went.

After a few moments he looked around and checked his handiwork, extending his senses and looking with spirit eyes. As he walked through into the healing room proper, he stopped. Pausing, he tuned in. Something felt wrong. Very wrong. Trusting his instincts, he scanned for the source. And looked up.

High in the sky a white glowing light, circular in shape, appeared in the distance. Staring intently the glowing form seemed to pulsate from within, as though active in some way.

As he watched the phenomenon it began to transform, swiftly becoming horizontal and lengthening in shape. The light intensified in the centre, changing colour slightly, and started to expand, as though a doorway was opening. The phenomenon stabilised. Then, in front of his eyes, reptiles started pouring out of the opening.

Mark stood transfixed for several moments as more and more reptiles poured out, forming a long line and staring down at him. Continuing to look up at the scene above, he could see what looked like another large group of reptile soldiers behind the first line, waiting to join the fray.

The full impact of what was happening quickly dawned on him. This was a small army of reptilians come to attack him in a brazen flouting of universal law and balance. A massive display of power. This was a revenge attack for him closing the conduit and taking away their portal and entrance into our realm.

He knew instinctively they wanted to re-establish that conduit and reassert their dominance in the process. If they got him out of the way they could reconnect the conduit, giving them free rein to travel between their world and ours uncontested.

Aggressive and territorial by nature, they were furious and had come for blood. His.

Angling their bodies forward, ready to sweep down and attack, Mark reacted fast. Energy flooded into his body at a tremendous rate. Holding his arms out at forty-five degrees he allowed the energy to build. Soldier guides appeared at his side and behind him. The huge light rock elemental that stood guard downstairs stepped behind him also, swiftly followed by his cosmic soldier, and guardian angel. Two more light elemental beings stepped up behind him, adding their power and support.

Brimming with light and power, Mark put one foot back to brace himself. His arms swept forward, releasing the pent-up energy, and a barrier of intense white light swept up towards the reptilian forces, the likes of which he had never seen before. The long line of pure crackling energy streaked across the sky and struck the now moving reptilians with tremendous force. Ripples of energy reverberated across the sky upon impact and their advance stopped dead.

Momentarily stunned, the reptilians recovered and pushed back, desperately trying to force a way past this new threat. Generating more power into the barrier, Mark grimaced with effort as he used every ounce of his strength to hold the attacking force at bay. He knew that even more reptilians were waiting on the other side of the portal to come through and that he could not afford to give way, even a fraction.

Lengthy seconds passed with no movement on either side. Then he felt the supporting energy of the beings around him increase and their boosted input giving him renewed strength.

With an explosive breath and using their combined might, he slowly began pushing the reptilians back towards the gateway. But it was taking everything he had, and the forced retreat was being fought every inch of the way. For what seemed an eternity the battle of strength continued between the two opposing forces. Then, out of nowhere, cosmic soldiers appeared alongside the reptilian attack force. More and more appeared, until the reptilian force was totally surrounded.

Mark watched as this unexpected cosmic force joined the fray countering the attack. The tide turned significantly in their favour as the reptile force was overwhelmed and rounded up. The cosmic soldiers started to take hold of the reptilians and drag them back through the portal whence they had come.

Standing in situ and keeping his energy in play, he realised that these cosmic beings had not suddenly just appeared by luck. They had been waiting for this to occur.

Dropping his arms to his side, but still heightened with residual power, Mark watched as the last of the reptile forces were taken away and the light gateway they had used vanished from sight.

As he turned around a cosmic being of obvious high rank stood in front of him.

A moment's pause ensued as they looked at each other. A slight off-white silvery colour and an almost alien-like quality exuded from the shiny being in front of him.

'Thank you,' it said. 'We have been after them for a long time.'

Nonplussed, Mark looked at it with silent questions. He had an idea of what was going on, but not much, and wanted answers.

As if reading his mind, the cosmic being answered.

'They are a rogue element within the reptile realm. We have been looking for them for a long time. Monitoring and waiting. You facilitated our being able to catch them. Thank you.'

Mark thought for a moment.

'You mean you used us to get to them?'

'Yes. Both you and Francesca. She is the portal that drew them in.'

Mark had a sense they could have done this without them, and sooner.

As if in answer to his unvoiced question the cosmic being answered.

'We could have done this earlier. But the big picture. It's part of your growth. Both of you.'

Intrinsically Mark understood this. Part of him still felt rankled about it. But that was ego, the still-human emotion part of him and swiftly he let it go.

'Who are you?'

'I am cosmic. Part of the great force that manages and looks after things on a much bigger scale. A universal scale. Earth is just one planet among many. We watch many solar systems and planets, all of which are under our eyes and jurisdiction.'

He looked carefully at Mark and spoke again. His voice was

light and had an alien quality to it.

'You have done well and we thank you for your help. This is not the first time you have helped us, but it is not your time to work fully with us yet. We will come in and out as needed. You are to focus your work on this planet for now. But we will be about and watching; your job here is not yet done.'

Clearly finished with his explanation, they looked at each other. And then, with a nod, the cosmic being vanished.

Mark stood still, mulling over what had just occurred. Then his spider sense tingled. As he was extending his senses a feeling of being watched came over him. Somewhere in the distant ether, a group of demon elders were sitting around a long wooden table, surreptitiously observing him. Watching, testing. Feeling secure from their hidden vantage point so far, far away.

But Mark had seen them. He looked up towards their faraway place and made his presence known, and spoke in a deadly tone.

'I see you. And I will come for you soon.'

The demon elders sat up wide-eyed and looked at each other in shock. Then vanished from sight.

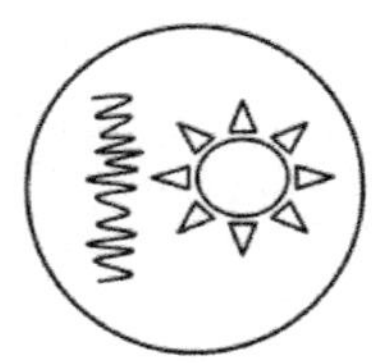

Chapter 41

The Demon Council

Later that night Mark was practising his Hua Tuo qi gong, an ancient Chinese practice used for self-healing and well-being. The focus and the exact result of the qi gong depends very much on the style of practice you choose (there are allegedly over one hundred thousand forms of qi gong in China).

Only in recent decades has it become more popular in the West. The majority are well-being forms, and while all qi gong practices do of course enhance well-being and energy flow, a smaller number are more specific in their goals and methods. Some of these goals potentially involve developing specific abilities for the practitioner, for example being able to use their qi or chi for things like healing for both themselves and others or for moving objects without physically touching them, manipulating the qi so that physical blows become far more powerful.

Or they can use their energy as a shield, strengthening and transforming it into a kind of physical body armour. This has been demonstrated publicly over the decades by groups such as the Shaolin monks, who demonstrate that blades and sharp pointed objects are unable to penetrate their skin, or move people without touching them.

Mark practised a rarer healing form of qi gong, which he had studied when young with an old Chinese master for over ten years, practising religiously every day. At that time it was almost unheard of in the UK. It was the backbone of his core energy development and strength, and had enabled him to manipulate energy in various forms, including healing for both people and animals.

As his body eased through the random movements he loosened his mind and observed previous events drifting through, allowing the answers to come. The cosmic forces were unexpected new players, but good ones.

For now he could put them to the side. The other new players who had also shown themselves, albeit unwittingly, were this group of demon elders. What was their role in all this? How long had they been involved? And why?

Everything was still escalating. Darkness was spreading. More and more cases were coming forward. Only the other day he had had to attend another victim of this rise in darkness. An old client of his who had dabbled in witchcraft and spiritual work had been ruthlessly attacked by a black magic cult. Her husband, at a loss for what to do and with limited knowledge of other-unworldly events, had called Mark in desperation, as conventional doctors had been unable to help.

He had immediately agreed, and travelled there the next day. On arrival he found her curled up on the back seat of her car, a quivering wreck, sobbing and crying incoherently.

Assessing the situation quickly he had been forced to take extreme action and had done something that he had never done before, something that cannot be done without permission from the higher powers. He had closed the doorways to her talent. But it had solved the problem and she had improved immediately. Her husband had called later that night with sincere gratitude, stating she was now much better and on the way to a full recovery. Yet this was only one case of so many coming to light.

And the demon elders … they were the significant new players. Mulling it over as he eased his way through his exercises, he came to a stop. Again he had that sense of being watched.

Cautiously he looked around. His gaze halted as he looked at the conservatory, his main healing room. It was pitch-black and Mark approached it with all his senses alert. Scanning the room as he entered, he was unable to pinpoint the source of his unease.

He turned and walked back into the main house, trying to dismiss the sensation of someone watching. Try as he might though, that nagging feeling just wouldn't go away. He just knew something was there. He turned around again and walked back into the healing room and flicked the light switch on. The darkness vanished as the bright LED bulbs cast their light across the room.

And there, standing right in from of him, was a large dark cloud of energy, rippling and swirling as though it were alive. Stopping dead where he was, his shields slid swiftly into place and energy flowed into him automatically.

Mark looked intently at the black cloud. It was not a cloud exactly, he realised, but rather a force powered by a collective group of demons behind it. A demon horde.

Simultaneously with that realisation his huge light elemental suddenly appeared next to him and Mark immediately stepped into his energy fields, merging and becoming one. This light elemental usually stood guard downstairs in his lounge. Similar to a rock troll with jagged white outlines and only vaguely humanoid in shape, it gave the impression of an enormous doorman, which in reality it was. Only exponentially more powerful.

Mark felt its power infuse him, and revelled in it. Two other light elementals appeared either side of him and to the rear, placing a second shield to the side and behind protecting his rear and flanks.

The cosmic mercenary who worked with Mark suddenly materialised in front of him, and powerful beams of white light shot out of his hands, slamming into the dark swirling mass. Instantly Mark drew power from all those with him and his own bolt of light shot out at the mass, merging and impacting at the same point as that of the cosmic mercenary.

With their combined strength the light blast hit with incredible power and the mass convulsing wildly where it struck. The light beams continued, relentless and unabated. Inhuman cries could be heard from within the mass as the sustained blast continued its unrelenting onslaught.

Mark could see dark shadowy forms inside the phenomenon, twisting and turning in pain, desperately trying to escape their torture. What had originally been their staging platform for an attack was now fast becoming their tomb. Trapped and in agony, the demonic horde within now frantically sought only to escape.

Seconds later a group of cosmic soldiers appeared out of nowhere and encircled the convulsing dark mass. Linking their energy they formed a tangible ring of silvery light around the mass, effectively blocking all escape. Once the ring was secure a cosmic contingent broke away from the main group and poured inside to deal with the horde.

Mark watched as the demons within were dragged away, to be dealt with by the powers that be. Within minutes all the would-be usurpers were removed, leaving the dark portal empty. The cosmic soldiers surrounding the mass exerted their power, slowly constricting the ring of energy. As he watched they forced the mass to gradually shrink, literally turning in upon itself, till long moments later it vanished completely as though it had never been.

Mark stepped back, still intoxicated with power, and looked about. The presence he sensed before had returned, and he looked up into the ether. There they were. The demon elders staring down from behind their table, observing. So they had masterminded this attack? Anger rose within him, amplified by the elemental guard whose energy field he now shared.

Mark focused his power and stepped out of his physical body, and moments later rematerialised in a large rock cavern some sixty feet long and forty feet wide. He gazed over his new surroundings. The cavern consisted of three levels. Halfway along the first level some stairs were cut into the rock leading up to the second level, which in turn went on for another twenty feet or so.

Four more steps carved into the rock led up to a raised dais supporting a long dark wooden table, behind which sat the six elder demons. For a few moments they stared across at each other, then a glowing shield of grey energy rose up in front of the second level, blocking Mark's path to the dais and them.

Shock and outrage showed on their features at his sudden appearance. With an unsaid gesture lower-level demons streamed out of nowhere and threw themselves at the invaders of their inner sanctum. Realisation swiftly dawned. These demon elders were behind all the unrest and chaos. The ones responsible for the attacks on him and his home. Anger and steely determination grew at this realisation. Thoughts of the attack he had just defeated mere moments before by the reptilian contingent sat freshly in his mind.

Glowing bright white and still infused with his light elemental, battle lust coursed through him and Mark eagerly stepped forward meeting them head on. Hands swept out and struck the attacking demons, sweeping them aside like a scythe through wheat. Some vanished on impact. Others spun away, smashed against the far walls or collapsing comatose on the floor, only to disappear seconds later. Resolutely he moved forward step by step, brushing aside the never-ending onslaught of demons who flung themselves at him to block his path.

Time and time again they threw themselves at him, but to no avail. Yet more and more came, joining the fray in a seemingly endless dark swathe streaming towards him. His forward movement slowed, grinding to a crawl as he was forced to deal with the never-ending dark tide of demons. But there were too many.

Through his battle-hazed vision he became aware of cosmic forces appearing by his side, combining their silvery powers with his own. Dark and light energy forms intermixed and the air crackled as sizzling bolts of power were exchanged from both sides. Dark forms were flung across the cavern popping on impact where they then vanished from sight. Others were knocked senseless while some were simply cut in half with bolts of light scathing through their ranks. The battle raged for minutes with no quarter given on either side, till eventually they stood alone before the dark grey energy barrier. Dark and light residue streamed from the walls and floor, and you could feel the air loaded with static charge.

The six demon elders sat behind the table, unmoving, looking at him. Even now, in their arrogance, they believed their shield to be impenetrable. But the cosmic beings standing next to him changed everything. Sweeping forward, they raised their arms as one, and with their combined might, silver and white energy beams struck the barrier with tremendous power.

The barrier shimmered and swirled frantically on impact.

Hues of grey and a multitude of other colours weaved across its surface as it struggled to withstand the blast. Suddenly there was an explosive sound within the ether and the shield vanished, the displaced energy flying through the air around them.

The elders were stunned and dazed. They had combined all their linked power to hold the shield in place. And the breaking of that shield had taken its toll.

Recovering moments later, realisation of their predicament dawned and they stood up, desperately looking for a way to escape. Still fully merged with his light elemental and enraged with battle intoxication, Mark was in no mood to let them escape. Raising his hands, light beams swiftly slammed into their ranks stunning them, and the cosmic soldiers were on them in an instant. Light streamed from his hands, wrapping around their throats, and held them all in a vice-like grip, rendering them impotent.

The six demon elders were now secured and pinned down, and Mark walked up to the dais and looked at them. Enhanced by the cosmic forces at his side and by the other beings working with him, there was nothing they could do. Helpless, fearful and angry all at the same time, the mixture of emotions played across their faces as they looked at him impotently.

'You made a mistake coming here and playing with me,' he said in a deadly tone.

As he held their gaze a deeper understanding came to him. This was a council of elders within the demonic realms. While powerful and secretly sanctioned by the upper hierarchy above them, those same ultimate powers would leave them to hang if they were unsuccessful in their endeavours.

The elders looked at him indignantly. Mark twisted his hands and the energy around their throat tightened and they remained silent.

Now fully in control, he stared at them for some moments and made a decision.

'You will be dealt with and you will answer for your crimes,' he said with a voice like granite, his eyes boring into their own. 'Don't ever come back again.'

After letting his words sink in for a moment he turned his head to the cosmic forces close by.

'Take them away,' he said out loud in disgust, gesturing disdainfully with one hand. And the elders vanished, along with a detachment of cosmic soldiers.

He scanned the cavern. It was unnaturally empty and silent, with no sign of the titanic battle that had raged across its depths just moments before. Only the residue static charge still simmering below the surface gave testimony.

With a final glance Mark disappeared and re-entered his body, sagging a little as he did so. The battles had sapped him more than he expected. He felt significantly drained due to losing the boost from his light elemental as it left him.

He placed his hand on the wall and paused for a few moments, then walked to the leather sofa and sat down gratefully.

Giving himself a few moments to recover he relaxed and let his thoughts move back over recent events. When he revisited the scene in his mind he instinctively knew that the demon elders were the driving force behind these events. Although they were not the ultimate mastermind behind it all they were big players, nevertheless, and he had taken them out.

For now that would do. Satisfied, he closed his eyes and fell immediately into a deep sleep.

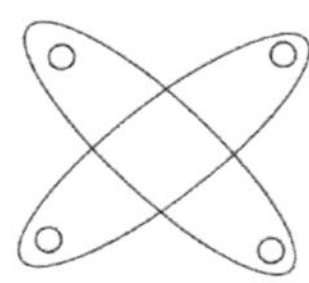

Chapter 42

Night Attack
Final Training

The next few weeks passed without incident and Mark settled down into the usual routine of things, enjoying the return to some semblance of normality. Whatever that may be in his world, some may observe.

On one such normal evening, having finished with his clients for the day and eaten, he settled down to watch one of his favourite recorded programmes on television. He was relaxed and engrossed in the middle of a particularly vivid scene when a loud thump sounded from above cutting through his focus. He frowned and paused the TV to listen, sitting silently for several long seconds straining to hear what it was, but no more sounds came and all was quiet. Yet it was just too loud to ignore.

Ever conscious of the strange world he lived in, but also aware that he lived in a house with two cats that could be up to mischief, he got up and walked upstairs to investigate. On reaching the landing he saw his cats fast asleep in their beds. His brow furrowed again. This obviously ruled out them jumping down from something and causing the loud thump on the ceiling. Tuning into his senses he felt outwards, aware that he could be looking for something else. Something non-physical.

On alert and ready, he stepped into his bedroom, which was directly above the lounge where the thump had come from and was immediately brought up short. Standing in front of the window overlooking the garden was a large black demon, standing utterly motionless and silent, and looking straight at him. Between six and seven feet tall, with a hard exoskeleton, it had curved horns on its head and glowing red eyes. Its stocky legs were slightly bent at the knees, and its powerful arms culminating in clawed hands stuck out from its torso in an aggressive stance.

Mark absorbed the scene in front of him. The demon's intensity was off the scale and you could have cut it with a knife.

He stopped dead in his tracks for a moment and quickly weighed up the situation. This was not a run of the mill demon. This was a demon bred for one thing and one thing only. Battle. Motionless, it bored into Mark's eyes, totally focused on its prey.

Silently Mark's shields slid down into place as he drew in his power. Buying precious moments of time to gather himself, he spoke directly to it.

'What do you want?' he asked, with no trace of weakness in his voice.

Stoically the demon stared back at him. A complete lack of compassion in any shape or form lay within its being. It was almost bereft of any thoughts, other than its single purpose for being there.

Its powerful limbs bunched and launched itself straight at him with its arms extended reaching for his throat. With long-practised speed and no small amount of self-preservation Mark's hands flashed up and bolts of white light struck it straight in the chest, almost halting its charge. But not quite. The demon's desire to reach its prey was all-consuming. Snarling, it pushed through the bolts of light and pain striving to reach him. Mark dug deep and reinforced light beams spun around its limbs and body, securing and halting its advance.

It fought like a madman, and its desire to reach its perceived prey was unrelenting. Placing one foot back to brace himself Mark took a deep breath and surged more power around the demon.

For some moments Mark held it at bay and then slowly started to push it back. But the process was far too slow, and any mistake would have dire consequences.

The cosmic mercenary who worked with him jumped into the fray and Mark embraced his power. Their combined energy forced the demon's backward motion to increase as it dug in its heels in response. Chillingly silent, red eyes boring into him, its ferocity was incredible, and every fibre of its being strained to break free and rip into him and tear him apart.

Always present and always on the alert, his huge light elemental guardian raced up from downstairs into the bedroom at terrific speed and slammed into the demon with tremendous impact. The energy reverberated across the room as the demon was knocked back several paces.

Quickly Mark summoned a portal to the underworld, which moments later appeared in his healing room below. Inky black and seemingly bottomless, it beckoned the demon on a journey into eternity. Increasing the intensity of his light beams with the combined power of the cosmic mercenary he steered it towards the waiting portal.

Raining terrible blows onto the demons body with club-like fists, the elemental ferocity of the guardian and its raw power tipped the balance, forcing the demon further and further back towards the ground until finally it hung over the edge of the portal. With one final mighty blow it toppled over the edge into the darkness beneath.

Thinking the job was done, Mark paused and started to turn away, but warning tingles travelled down his neck and he swung back to the as yet unclosed portal. The demon was trying to drag its way out. Two clawed hands were hooked onto the edge of the portal as it tried to climb back out. Renewing his assault, Mark blocked the entrance with a shield of light before it could get a purchase, battering its rising head as he did so. Its upward climb halted as it struck the barrier, and Mark called out to the underworld guardians with his spirit voice.

'This is your problem now. Take it away.'

A whispered groaning sound came from within the portal and dark hands reached up and dragged the maniacal battle demon back down into the underworld. Its clawed hands finally disappeared from sight.

Mark's elemental guardian dropped back down to the floor below and he took stock. Walking back downstairs, still fully tuned in, he looked around, extending his senses and scanning. Glancing up with spirit eyes to the sky above, he saw what appeared to be a black cloud. As he walked into his healing room he looked through the glass walls and roof, staring intently at it. Larger and closer than he had first thought, it was not that far away at all. And, this close to it, Mark could clearly see some sort of activity within.

Quickly he realised this was a second assault wave, and undoubtedly another demon attack force. Similar to the one before, but also different, in some crucial way he couldn't put his finger on. He needed to act swiftly before it stabilised and the second wave could cross over and renew their assault.

Immediately he began absorbing universal light and energy, rapidly ramping up his power levels as the energy flowed through and around him. Already tired, he had to act fast.

Raising his arms he threw out a barrier of light that streamed across the sky and encircled the black demonic cloud. Grimacing with effort, Mark strained to hold the barrier in place as the cloud pushed against his hastily erected barrier, flexing and moving within as though ready to break. Calling in his cosmic soldier to merge with him again fully the barrier stabilised, but it was still not enough.

Spirit guides rushed to his aid, joining the ranks of light to fight the threatening demonic attack force. Light spirit after light spirit joined the fray, and the forward motion of the cloud eventually halted. It swirled and convulsed within, but the containment field held.

Absorbing as much power as he could muster and straining every fibre of his being, he dug his heels in and threw everything he had at the barrier. But even with the combined forces at his side, it was not enough. And Mark knew it.

Between gritted teeth he called out to the universe for help.

Moments later a flash of intense blue light coalesced next to him, and Archangel Michael appeared by his side. Immediately he stepped into Mark's form and took control. Brilliant light shone from within him, brighter and with an intensity he had never seen before, as Mark embraced and fully accepted the archangel's power. Rather than being merely a passive observer, this time Mark retained a greater connection to himself. Intimately connected in a way that he had never previously experienced, he revelled in the euphoria he felt whilst within Archangel Michael's energy field.

Michael's power was awesome, and while Mark had witnessed him in action before this was different. He was almost untethered. Swiftly Michael's power swamped him as he exerted more control over his body, and Mark knew he was only feeling part of it. Any more and his human and energetic form would not be able to withstand it.

The power building up reached an intoxicating level, and his hair stood on end as his body swelled till he felt he would explode. Then, just at the point where he could take no more, Michael/ Mark raised his arms wide and slammed his hands together with earth shattering force.

Mark was stunned as a massive thunderclap ripped across the surrounding area. Dizziness threatened to swamp him and he was forced to close his eyes due to the sheer power of the explosion. The shock waves reverberated across the sky and streamed towards the dark mass. He waited several seconds for the energy wave to disperse. Opening his eyes he looked up.

The demonic cloud was gone.

Michael stepped out of Mark who then swayed against the wall, putting a hand out to steady himself. He looked up where Michael stood to his side a few feet away, glowing blue.

Gathering himself, Mark tried to think things through and make sense of the pandemonium that had just occurred. What had just happened and why? Michael had been absent for some time, and all Mark's attention and training had seemed to be focusing more on cosmic powers and other realms. He had thought that Michael was not so much involved in this. And why this sudden premeditated attack after weeks of calm? He thought that it was over for now. The battle won.

Frowning slightly in thought, Mark framed the question.

'Why?' he asked.

Looking pensive, Michael answered,

'To test you.'

Dumbly Mark asked again.

'Why?'

Michael stayed silent, watching him, forcing Mark to work it out for himself. And then he understood. The understanding slowly dawned on him as he put the pieces together. He was being tested to see if under extreme circumstances like this he would use darkness.

He hadn't.

Speaking again in frustration, craving more answers, he said,

'I thought you were not so involved in matters more cosmic.'

Michael answered in a gentle but powerful voice.

'You needed to know more again. Your training was focused on other matters needed for your training. I do indeed focus more on this planet, on solar systems and other planets close to us. But not only on them.

'You needed to be brought more knowledge. Made more aware. My power is such I can do this. You needed to see. Now you have been brought back to reality.'

Michael paused and looked not unkindly at him.

'It is hard for you to understand, but this is the way of things.'

Mark thought for a moment again. Understanding came to him. This was his final test. To see if he would use darkness or light. What would be his default instant reaction when pushed? But he had used light. He hadn't used darkness.

A sense of satisfied self-acknowledgement came over him and his shoulders dropped. Knowing he had been understood, Michael nodded and vanished.

Mark sighed as relief gently wafted through his body. He had passed the test.

Chapter 43

Answers

Mark was sitting on his favourite chair, meditating.

'Who are you?' he asked, as a glowing being of an origin Mark knew instinctively was one of power and secrecy appeared in front of him.

The being stood and, holding his gaze, looked at Mark. About six and a half feet tall, in humanoid form, there was an ethereal glow around him that reminded Mark of power and something else. Somewhere else. Above the normal spirit beings.

His arms were crossed, he looked stern, with an intimidating expression on his face and a commanding manner. But Mark knew instinctively he was not hostile and meant no harm. Clearly used to power, it emanated from him strongly as he answered.

'I serve a greater purpose. A greater power, if you like. We deal with, among other things, the balance of light and dark. The balance of light and dark must be maintained. You have been training for this purpose.'

'All this has been training?' Mark asked.

'Yes. This is the grand scheme of things, beyond which you do not know about.' The enigmatic being in front of him paused briefly in thought. 'Hmm. Well, you do now. Some of it, at least.'

Staring somewhere deep beyond, he paused again for a

moment. Then turned his eyes back to Mark and fixed him with a penetrating stare.

'We have sent you tests to deal with to continue your training. If you were to serve our purpose as a soldier of light in physical form then you needed to up your game. Few are chosen. Few survive.

'There is much you don't know. But, for now, know this. We are well pleased with you. You have done well.'

'And now?' Mark asked.

'Now? Now you have been given access to both light and dark. Not until you had proved you could work with light over dark and resist the allure of the dark could we allow this. Training you towards the dark was not so difficult, in some ways. It appealed to your nature. But it's a delicate balance.'

Mark answered with genuine feeling.

'I could feel the constant pull towards the dark. The way they are. The allure of them. I always had to bring myself back. It was like walking on a fence. It still is.'

'We know. But you were chosen because you are a born warrior. You have been many warriors in past lives. With this comes certain … traits. There are those traits that make you good at what you do but they also can lead you into darkness.

'Once you were proficient enough at working with them, we forced a change. It wasn't till you proved yourself proficient in light warfare, choosing light first and able to let go of the darkness, that you passed. Now you are ready and able to access both light and dark as needed. You have done well, and this part of your journey is over.'

'And what now?' Mark asked.

Red Shaman paused and looked at him.

'Now?' he replied. 'Now you serve.'

Epilogue

Since the writing of this book new powers have been given, new beings have been worked with and more journeys, experiences and growth have unfolded. Greater heights have been achieved even while writing this. Mark continues to grow and evolve and is being shown things that, despite everything he has already seen, continue to surprise him.

He is always honing his skills and becoming more powerful as time goes by. But he recognises now that no matter how much he learns there is so much more that he hasn't yet learnt. So very much more.

Mark is always in the service of the greater good and always answers the call of spirit, although much of his work goes unseen and unknown by the masses. But that does not matter. What matters is that Mark keeps working. And will continue to do so for as long as he is able to in this physical body. One suspects that will not stop once he is returned to his spirit form. But that is another story altogether.

ABOUT THE AUTHOR.

David Walther was born in West London. His early career was spent serving in various roles within the public sector.

In 1996 David began studying Hua Tuo Qi Gong, a rarer form of self-healing Qi Gong, under a Chinese master who had moved to England from China. This was his first introduction into Chi energy. At first this came in the form of self healing but it wasn't long before David was able to transmit Chi himself.

In 2006 David started his spiritual journey in earnest, learning from many teachers, and was soon fast tracked by spirit. This enabled him to help others to greater effect with an expanding repertoire of abilities, which are still continuously growing and improving today. Now living in Surrey, David continues to learn and evolve whilst teaching and helping others.

Find out more about David and his work here :
www.davidwalther.co

Printed in Great Britain
by Amazon